THE FATHERLAND A

'Wiener was not just uncannily prescient about German history. By taking hate speech seriously, he created a remarkably fresh and fine-grained picture of the politics of enmity, making him relevant and inspirational for historians of our own present'

Joseph Leo Koerner, Victor S. Thomas Professor of History of Art and Architecture and Creative Director of the Vienna Project, Harvard University

'Passionate, yet thoroughly documented, Alfred Wiener's pamphlets, written just after the Great War, are both fascinating and uncanny'

Lisa Appignanesi, author of *Everyday Madness: On Grief, Anger, Loss and Love*

'Warning in 1919 that lies and conspiracy theories about Jews would lead to pogroms, Alfred Wiener foretold events that would lead to the destruction of democracy in Germany and the annihilation of Europe's Jews. His words carry lessons for our time as well'

Ruth Ben-Ghiat, author of *Strongmen: from Mussolini to the Present*

'A chilling eye-opener. This beautifully introduced and carefully annotated study will intellectually enlighten and arm those who seek to understand and halt the dark machinations of xenophobic hatred and antisemitism in our day'

Wendy Lower, author of *Hitler's Furies: German Women in the Nazi Killing Fields*, Director of the Mgrublian Center for Human Rights at Claremont McKenna College, and Chair of the Academic Committee of the US Holocaust Memorial Museum

The Fatherland and the Jews

TWO PAMPHLETS BY ALFRED WIENER,
1919 AND 1924

Alfred Wiener

Translated from the German and annotated by Ben Barkow
Introduction and Afterword by Michael Berkowitz
Foreword by Daniel Finkelstein

A COLLABORATION BETWEEN
THE WIENER HOLOCAUST LIBRARY
AND GRANTA BOOKS

GRANTA

Granta Publications, 12 Addison Avenue, London, W11 4QR

First published in Great Britain by Granta Books, 2021

Prelude to Pogroms?: Facts for Thoughtful People was originally
published in German in 1919 as *Vor Pogromen?: Tatsachen für Nachdenkliche*
by Verlag 'Gabriel Rießer', Berlin SW68 Lindenstr. 13.

German Jewry in Political, Economic and Cultural Perspective was a lecture
given to the Deputy Syndic of the Central Association of German Citizens
of Jewish Faith in Dessau on 25 January 1924 and was originally published
in German as *Das deutsche Judentum in politischer, wirtschaftlicher und kultureller
Hinsicht* by Philo Verlag, Berlin SW68, Lindenstraße 13.

The publication of this work was made
possible through a grant from the Granta Trust.

A CIP catalogue record is available from the British Library

2   4   6   8   9   7   5   3   1

ISBN 978 1 78378 621 3
eISBN 978 1 78378 622 0

Typeset in Bembo by Patty Rennie
Printed and bound in Great Britain by T J Books, Padstow

www.granta.com

THE FATHERLAND AND THE JEWS

Contents

Foreword

by Daniel Finkelstein

WHEN ALFRED WIENER died in 1964, I had yet to reach my second birthday, so I suppose in any normal sense of the word I didn't really know my grandfather at all. I've had to make do with being told that in his last months he loved holding me, and yet I feel I know him well, and that his spirit is with me always.

You have in your hands the products of the thoughts and political instincts of an extraordinary man. Someone who could see what others could not see, and acted when others did not act.

Here's what he understood. First that ideas matter. Even, perhaps especially, the deranged ravings of fringe groups and misfits. He saw that ideas precede action and that the notion that 'sticks and stones can break your bones, but words can never hurt you' is a deeply foolish one. Before sticks and stones there are always words, and that's why we have to take the words seriously.

Second, and proceeding from that broad principle, he understood what was happening in Germany, he had an instinct for the words he was hearing and the people he was hearing them from. Perhaps the most impressive single thing in this publication is the date. To have glimpsed his country's future as early as 1919 and 1924 was insight of a rare kind.

What makes it more impressive still, but also more tragic, is that he admitted to himself and told others a truth he deeply wanted not to be true. Not simply because if it was true it posed a physical threat, but because it went against all that he held dear, and all he thought was possible.

Alfred Wiener loved Germany. He argued that the future for the Jewish community was there, not in Palestine. To be so passionately committed to this idea of German Jewry and yet, simultaneously, so capable of appreciating that it was in peril, was a rare gift.

My grandfather understood something else. He could see that lies had to be fought with truth. If ideas matter, then it is vital to collect evidence that challenges bad ideas and supports good ones. What led him to begin his library was not a librarian's temperament, even though he loved books and was somewhat of a hoarder. He started it because he was an activist and a journalist.

In the same way, this book is not the work of a stylist or

a wit, even though by all accounts Alfred Wiener could be extremely droll. It is primarily a piece of reporting. And not a neutral piece either. He is sounding an alarm, albeit one that too few people heard and even fewer heeded.

Let us hope it is heard now. Historians will want to read this book, and it will hopefully influence their understanding of how the Holocaust took shape. But I hope others will take heed of it too.

For if there was ever a moment in the post-war era when it is necessary to remind people of how actions flow from bad ideas and how the unhinged theories of conspiracists and bigots threatens liberty and peace, that moment is now.

I hope it is all right to add a further note. More personal this time. What is contained here is not the writing of a disinterested observer. What Alfred Wiener foresaw in this book came to pass and it engulfed him.

It killed my grandmother; it starved my mother and her sisters almost to death; it made them all stateless, homeless and propertyless.

Perhaps you have read before – indeed, I am sure you have – Holocaust witness statements after the fact. What makes this book special is that it is a witness statement before the fact.

Introduction

by Michael Berkowitz

ALFRED WIENER WAS born in 1885 into the heyday of Wilhelmine Germany, the (second) German Empire, or *Kaiserreich*.[1] The Great War (1914–18, later the First World War) would be the undoing of that age. Elements of Wiener's life – material comfort, a broadly humanistic education and travel abroad – were shared by many German Jews. His family ran a thriving haberdashery and hat store. They lived in Potsdam, an august garrison town outside of Berlin. Due to his family's business interests, Wiener partly grew up in Bentschen, in an eastern province of the German Empire, which ceded to Poland after the First World War.

After attending grammar school in Bentschen, Wiener finished his secondary education in Postdam, and then studied at the universities of Berlin and Heidelberg. He took courses at Berlin's Hochschule für die Wissenschaft des Judentums, the Institute for Advanced Academic Jewish Studies.[2] Wiener contemplated, but decided against becoming a rabbi. He also studied 'oriental' languages, philosophy and history. In 1907, in his early twenties, he was advised to visit Italy as a rest cure after a bout of influenza. He passed through Italy, but spent the bulk of his time in Egypt, and travelled to Palestine and Syria.[3]

Alfred Wiener decided to undertake research in Arabic literature of the ninth and tenth centuries, attaining his doctorate in Heidelberg in 1913. His stated topic, the genre *al-faraj ba'd al-shiddah* ('relief after hardship'), included authors al-Tanukhi, al-Mada'ini, and Ibn Abi al-Dunya. The volume of al-Tanukhi 'comprises fourteen chapters of stories (of past communities and prophets) and traditions dealing with various hardships (such as hunger, being robbed, and having incurred the wrath of a ruler), and gives advice about how to be patient and face difficulties in life'.[4] There is a confluence between Alfred Wiener's passion for this school of medieval Arabic literature, his advocacy of humanitarianism and tolerance and his role as progenitor of one of the world's foremost research bodies in the service of human rights.

Wiener would maintain his interest in the Middle East, taking an anti-Zionist position in a thoughtful book and articles about Zionist settlement and Jewish-Arab relations in the 1920s. He did not see Zionism, as an incipient national movement, as promising a sufficient or practical response to the crises faced by European Jewry.[5]

There was not much time between what Wiener must have thought of as the launch of his academic career in 1913–14, and being drafted into the German army. Around the time he finished his PhD and began his military service in 1915, he was hired as an assistant to Paul Nathan (1857–1927). Nathan edited a liberal periodical, *Die Nation*, and, more famously, was a founder of the Hilfsverein, an organization concerned with enhancing the political position and educational opportunities for Jews in the Balkans and Near East, including Palestine.[6] Because the Hilfsverein used German in its projects and schools, it ran foul of the Zionists in Palestine, who were intent on reviving Hebrew and using it in daily life.[7]

After receiving basic training, Wiener joined the German army's infantry and saw action in both eastern and western theatres of the Great War. Knowing Arabic and Turkish, he served as a translator in the Ottoman campaign, and survived clashes with heavy casualties, including the Battle of Katia (23 April 1916), Romani on the Suez Canal (4 August 1916) and Bir-el Abd in the Sinai (9 August 1916). He was assigned to the educational unit (Lehrkommando) among soldiers deploying heavy artillery in late 1916. After suffering nearly fatal bouts of dysentery, he administered and edited an army newspaper, *Yildirim*, from posts in Jerusalem and Damascus, cities he knew from his earlier travels. He was also commissioned to write news items and pamphlets on 'cultural and historical topics to educate the army'.[8] He was awarded the Iron Cross, Second Class, and the Iron Crescent, for those who had served in the Near East.

In 1918 Germany suffered an agonizing defeat. The term 'stalemate' is batted around so automatically it is possible to forget that the Central Powers lost a war they really did desperately seek to win. The end of the *Kaiserreich* combined elements of both disintegration and revolution. 'They called it a revolution,' journalist Stefan Lorant later reflected. 'But was it really? There was no one – with the possible exception of Karl Liebknecht and Rosa Luxemburg on the extreme left – ready to lead the masses, ready to formulate their aims, ready to outline a new order in place of the old.'[9]

The break-up of the old regime was ignited by a naval mutiny at the end of October 1918. Rioting, spurred by returning soldiers and sailors, spread across Germany, and by 9 November the Kaiser was pressed to abdicate. He fled, in disguise. The uprisings were crushed with a large measure of gratuitous violence by right-wing mercenaries, the so-called Freikorps (Free Corps), who had been hired by Weimar's Social Democratic government. These squads, typically led by ex-army officers, included soldiers who refused to disband, often armed with army-issue weapons.[10]

The early Freikorps victims included anarchist Gustav Landauer, who was murdered during the suppression of the short-lived, utopian Bavarian Socialist Republic in 1919. Landauer's brand of anarchism, which also counted an ardent base in London's East End and New York's Lower East Side, proposed a society devoid of any form of exploitation and coercion. A small but passionate following in Central Europe, inspired by Landauer's idea of 'communitarian socialism',[11] included Gershom Scholem, Martin Buber and Hans Kohn, exceptionally creative minds in the fledgling Zionist movement.[12] Erich Fromm, a psychoanalyst and pioneer of social psychology associated with the Institute of Social Research, known in its American incarnation as the Frankfurt School, also upheld the legacy of Landauer.[13]

Despite massive loss of life and hundreds of thousands of wounded men, many people resisted accepting defeat in 1918. German cities, towns and villages had been spared from the war. Anguish over the defeat was dramatically embittered because only months before the German collapse it seemed that the sacrifice of war might have been worthwhile: Germany was set to gain vast amounts of territory, with bountiful farmland and diverse natural resources, through the Brest-Litovsk Treaty (3 March 1918), negotiated with the new Bolshevik masters of the old Russian Empire. German generals and the landed gentry unfurled grand plans, and prematurely luxuriated in their conquest. In a rousing beer-hall speech of 31 May 1921, Adolf Hitler contrasted the humiliating conditions of the Versailles Treaty with the supposedly generous terms that Germany had offered to a crippled Russia in 1918.[14] Fairness and generosity, to be sure, was in the eye of the beholder. When a nation surrenders, however, such wartime deals go up in smoke.

These circumstances contributed to the mistaken belief that Germany had been 'stabbed in the back', rather than losing a war,[15] a convention so well rehearsed that Wiener didn't have to raise it explicitly in his writings of 1919 and 1924. In his recent scholarly biography of Adolf Hitler, Brendan Simms asserts that the United States was part of Hitler's plans well in advance of the Second World War itself. The United States forces had, after all, tipped the balance of the tortuous, drawn-out war for the Allies in 1917. The soldier who would become *Der Führer* seethed with fury at America, which he increasingly believed to be tainted by malign Jewish influence. Hitler coveted not only disputed Danzig (Gdansk) and the 'Polish corridor', expansive *Lebensraum* (living space) in the east (including Ukraine) and European-wide domination, but also the *coup de grâce* of bringing the United States to its knees.[16]

After the armistice, Alfred Wiener became an official for the Centralverein deutscher Staatsbürger jüdischen Glaubens, CV or Centralverein (the Central Association of German Citizens of Jewish Faith). The CV was, by far, the largest and most comprehensive body dealing with the lives of German Jewry. He became the deputy chairman of the CV and eventually editor of its newspaper, the *CV Zeitung*.[17]

It was not simply antisemitism, per se, that moved Alfred Wiener to begin gathering material and speaking about the far-right and racist polemics that started appearing, in great abundance, after Germany's defeat in the Great War.[18] It was the *völkisch*, irrational character of this matter, not the anti-Jewish hatred only, that Wiener found so unsettling. *Volk* here, loosely meaning 'folk' and *völkisch*, 'popular', also signify a connection to an imagined primordial national essence. Everyone knew that antisemitism had long existed, and most likely always would, as it was a protean element of Christian mythologies. But what Wiener was seeing, reading and hearing since the defeat in 1918 seemed to be of a different order.

In the first of these publications, *Prelude to Pogroms?: Facts for Thoughtful People* (1919), Alfred Wiener revealed evidence of the systematic dissemination of antisemitic propaganda. Why are stories, he asked, which are contrary to known recent

events, to the rules of cause and effect and to indisputable scientific knowledge, so avidly amplified?[19] Wiener wished to
expose the scale of this deluge of 'leaflets, pamphlets, handbills and stickers', some with print runs in the millions, and
the financiers of this propaganda machinery, including weekly
magazines and daily newspapers.[20] He was aghast that '[t]he
great public' – even beyond the people who chose to read this
material – 'do not escape "education". Individuals are paid to
speak on the streets, in the trams, the trains and the elevated
railway – not only in Berlin – to stir things up.'[21]

Wiener sought to inform his listeners and readers about a
stream of anti-Jewish agitation that did not seem to be taken
seriously. It was rubbish, obviously, peddled by crackpots and
nonentities, but people were reading it, and some of this idiocy
was being repeated and popping up elsewhere as 'fact'. Can't
everyone see, he asked, that this isn't simply left versus right,
squabbling between the usual parties or factional dissent, played
(however roughly) by the old rules of the game?[22] Why were
these lies and libels embraced and touted by conservatives, who
claimed to be 'Fighters for the Truth'?[23] Why were so few will-
ing to challenge these baseless rants, as they seeped into print,
creeping into every village, town and city square, champi-
oned by men brandishing weapons? 'When they are not being
observed,' we learn, 'they speak openly about the desirability

of plundering Jewish businesses, of murder and manslaughter.'[24]

Wiener argues that this nonsensical propaganda may seem random and chaotic.[25] But, he contended, racism fused with ultra-nationalism, an obsession with opposition between 'the Jews' and idealizing fantasies of 'the Aryan' and 'pure German blood', was an existential threat.[26] He tried reason. In the face of incessant talk of 'Jewish conspiracy', he calmly explained that "[t]here is no such thing as a somehow unified, supranational Jewish organization, nor could there be'.[27]

Racist tracts also took swipes at 'Slavs', Asians, Africans and other nations. Among the only 'enviable' traits of Poles and Romanians, according to the *völkisch* writers, is their lust for anti-Jewish pogroms,[28] most famously in 1881, 1903 and 1905, and recently seen in antisemitic massacres in the Russian civil war (1917), and subsequent border wars involving Poland and Ukraine.

The *Münchner Beobachter* (*Munich Observer*), Wiener reported, 'believes it is not only the Jewish spirit, but also the Jesuit one, that rules Germany now'. Despite Catholics being vilified, hounded under Bismarck in the *Kulturkampf* of the 1870s,[29] they too could spread antisemitic abuse, as exemplified by the weekly *Leo* of Paderborn. 'Even *Germania*, the leading organ of the [Catholic] Centre Party', indulges in equating 'Jews and Spartacists', the most violent of Communists.[30] As a consequence of the raucous founding congress of the German Communist Party (KPD) (30 December 1918 to 1 January 1919), the divisions on the left hardened.[31]

Jew-hatred, long extant, was now conjured under the rubric of *völkisch* nationalism. Wiener perceived that otherwise disparate slogans, plaints and remedies were invariably transformed into blaming one's enemies, internal and external, but mainly 'the Jews', for all of Germany's woes. Jews, as people, and Judaism, a religion (as its enemies conceived it), were under attack.[32] These views were not, he thought, maintained by most non-Jewish Germans, and there were sensible, constructive, even brilliant correctives on offer.[33] But why had the flames not been smothered at their first surge? If Germans, overall, desired to get the country back on a stable footing, alas, 'to make Germany great again' after the Great War,[34] why this insipid yammering, and rivers of printers' ink spilled over 'race' and 'the Jews'? Something was going horribly off the rails, with a disturbing pattern to it. Wiener was drawing attention, as well, to the outrageous 'pan-German' territorial appetites the *völkisch* agitators displayed, which extended beyond 'revising' the dictates of Versailles.[35] This wasn't just the standard sabre-rattling. German incursions into the disputed territories it desired, maybe threats alone, would likely trigger incitement of pogroms.

Wiener did not feel obliged to remind his audiences that

the Weimar Republic was propped up on tenuous foundations, with sworn enemies exploiting any opportunity to undermine it. Recriminations, economic deprivation and despair would ensue.[36] And it wasn't all a partisan matter. Most Germans found their nation's treatment at Versailles appalling and unjust, which was seconded by the so-called 'Jewish' liberal dailies of the Mosses and the Ullsteins, respectively the *Berliner Tageblatt* and the *Frankfurter Zeitung*.[37] Nearly all Germans, not just those of the right, were angered by the 'war guilt' clause and reparations payments that seemed insurmountable. Hyperinflation and 'panic' were no good for anyone. Differences arose, though, over how best to respond to the bad hand the Germans were dealt, and the compounded crises.

The government earnestly sought ways to minimize ongoing strife, feed its population and restore industrial capacity. This was never going to be easy, with hardship and uncertainty dogging its efforts. Yet there was a fervent following for one of the Republic's most skilful public servants, Walther Rathenau (1867–1922).[38] As Minister of Reconstruction in 1921, he negotiated a significant alteration of the reparations, allowing for payments in kind to former adversaries. And as foreign minister he concluded the Rapallo Treaty (1922) with the Soviet Union, an important step in relieving Germany of its international isolation.[39] The diary kept by teenager Sebastian Haffner relates that Rathenau was the only politician in the Weimar Republic to have 'deeply stirred the imagination of young people and the masses'. Politicians, he wrote, such as Gustav Stresemann and Heinrich Brüning, 'who enjoyed longer periods of power and whose polices could be said to have moulded two brief periods of history, never radiated the same personal charisma' as did Rathenau:[40]

> It was not just politics. Rathenau's face appeared in the illustrated papers, like that of other politicians. The others were soon forgotten, but his face seemed to look straight at you and was difficult to forget, with its dark eyes full of intelligence and sadness. One read his speeches and behind the words one heard an unmistakable tone of reproach, challenge and promise: the tone of a prophet. [In his books] one sensed that dark emotional appeal, something both compelling and persuasive, challenging and seductive. They were at once restrained and fantastic, sobering and stirring, sceptical and enthusiastic. They spoke the bravest words in the most hesitant and gentle voice.[41]

During the war years, Rathenau had helped keep Germany from disintegration. But as a super-wealthy and prominent

Jew, committed to the nation emerging as a viable, peaceful republic, he was the *völkisch* crowd's most hated figure. Upon his appointment as foreign minister, right-wing fanatics yelled and chanted: '*Knallt ab den Walther Rathenau, die gottverdammte Judensau!*' ['Shoot down Walther Rathenau, the goddamned Jewish swine!'].

As Rathenau was being driven down the Königsallee in Berlin on 24 June 1922 in an open limousine, a car sped past. Boys from the *Völkisch* Defensive and Offensive League threw a hand grenade and sprayed Rathenau with automatic gunfire. He died within hours of the attack.[42]

A year earlier, the same faction had assassinated Matthias Erzberger (1875–1921) of the Catholic Centre Party, the Weimar government's finance minister.[43] On 24 November 1921, before an audience of 2,000 in Munich's Hofbräuhaus, Adolf Hitler fulminated against Erzberger as 'the greatest scoundrel who betrayed the Fatherland' in signing the Armistice, and added: 'We refuse to negotiate with the Jews. I prefer one hundred niggers in the beer hall to one single Jew.' This arresting summary of Hitler's view on 'race' prompted uproarious laughter from his listeners.[44] Some seven months earlier Hitler had resigned from the Reichswehr, the German army, but he continued to be paid through secret Reichswehr funds, despite the fact that the Reich supposedly no longer existed.[45]

'Instead of creating a people's army,' critic Siegfried Kracauer recalled in 1947, the early Weimar government had 'relied on the antidemocratic Freikorps formations to crush Spartacus', the far left. 'On January 15, 1919, Freikorps officers murdered Rosa Luxemburg, Karl Liebknecht – a crime soon followed by the series of notorious *Feme*[*Fehme*]-murders, not one of which was ever punished.'[46] These murders, historian George L. Mosse writes, were ordered by clandestine 'courts' taking law and order into their own hands, and usually perpetrated by teenagers. Erzberger, along with Rathenau, 'the Jews', Socialists and Communists, were blamed for Germany's surrender.[47]

Targeted political murders were not pogroms. But these actions, 'manslaughter' committed by former soldiers and their accomplices, who were supposed to have dispersed since the failed 'Kapp Putsch' of March 1920, were the kind of social violence that Wiener feared.[48] In the Kapp Putsch, German army officers with Freikorps gangs attempted to overthrow the tottering Weimar Republic to install an autocracy in the spirit of the *Kaiserreich*. Wiener had no sympathy for a Communist insurrection as a foil to the far right. But the murder of Luxemburg and Liebknecht, their bodies dumped in Berlin's Landwehr Canal, set an abhorrent precedent.

*

The murder of Walther Rathenau (June, 1922) is one of two major events absent from the second of Wiener's pamphlets printed in this book, from a lecture on 25 January 1924. In addition to the assassination of Rathenau, which some believed hurt the cause of the *völkisch* mob, Wiener did not address Hitler's 1923 Munich 'Beer Hall Putsch', in which the fledgling Nazi Party lost sixteen of its members.

Germany's post-war revolutions and reactions were taking ever more bizarre and frightening forms. Exceptionally odd ideas were stirring in Germany, talked about in hundreds of publications and beer-hall meetings and gaining traction. Before 1914, highly emotional 'romantic nationalism' seemed confined to outlandish mystics, cranks and oddballs that couldn't possibly be conceived as national political leaders. The refugee historian, Fritz Stern (1926–2016), referred to these trends as *The Politics of Cultural Despair* (1961); his contemporary, George Mosse (1918–99), contemplating a wider range of sources (including oral history) called the phenomena *The Crisis of German Ideology* (1964).[49]

After Mosse's book was published, some demeaned it as a 'catalogue of crackpots' or 'carnival of kooks' that didn't seem to be proper intellectual history. Surely Hitlerism proved that Germany had taken a horrific turn. But could this *völkisch* stream of nationalism really have been the incubator and engine of Nazism?[50] Mosse had relied, overwhelmingly, on printed material in London's Wiener Library that Alfred Wiener had recognized as significant – despite being, well, rubbish. It was, he said, 'where the spade work' for *The Crisis of German Ideology* was done. Mosse graciously thanked the librarian, Ilse R. Wolff (1908–2001), herself a refugee historian who deserves scholarly attention, 'who put her vast knowledge freely at my disposal'. He concluded, rather unusually: 'To the Wiener Library in London, truly a scholars' home, I wish to dedicate this book.'[51] Perhaps unsurprisingly, given his familiarity with and esteem for the institution, Mosse, a professor at the University of Wisconsin, was considered as a potential director of the Wiener Library in the early 1960s.[52] Later he held an ongoing visiting appointment at the Hebrew University of Jerusalem, and remained actively engaged in the work of the Wiener Library in both London and Tel Aviv.

The *völkisch* nationalism explicated by Mosse had represented to Alfred Wiener, as he was observing it, a kind of mystical, quasi-religious – and highly dangerous – sect, fusing racism and apocalyptic visions. Mosse was the first to revisit this idea, as an academic historian, after the war. Saul Friedländer would re-emphasize this critical dimension of Nazism by describing it as '"redemptive" antisemitism.'[53] Another significant founder of a research library and institute that eventually relocated from Nazi Germany to London was Aby Warburg (1866–1929). Warburg's endeavours were mainly focused on art history from antiquity through the Renaissance.[54] But like Alfred Wiener, Aby Warburg believed that there was something odd, deeply unsettling and 'mythological' about the antisemitic vitriol circulating in Hamburg since around 1900, re-energized in 1918. The books and pamphlets Warburg saved sit on a few shelves of the Warburg Institute library, in Woburn Square, which is almost within shouting distance from the Russell Square home of the Wiener Holocaust Library.

Prelude to Pogroms?: Facts for Thoughtful People specified many of the names and organizations that would serve as a roadmap for Mosse's *Crisis of German Ideology*. As an overarching theme, Wiener articulated his fear that the unrestrained fervour that unleashed pogroms, wanton destruction and violence perpetrated on hundreds of Jewish communities in the Russian Empire[55] might be repeated in vanquished Germany. While widespread pogroms did *not* occur in Germany in the early 1920s, antisemitism, including assault and murder, became firmly enmeshed in the political landscape. Prior to the start of the Second World War, coordinated mass violence against Jews, including the burning of most of Germany's synagogues, occurred in the wake of the Austrian Anschluss in March

1938, and during Kristallnacht, the night of broken glass, of 9 and 10 November 1938.[56] Although the term 'pogrom' persists as another name for Kristallnacht, it should not be called a pogrom: François Guesnet and Uli Baumann argue that because it was clearly directed by the highest Nazi authorities, and blanketed the entire nation, it had little of the grass-roots and scatter-shot character of the pogroms in Eastern Europe.[57]

The absence of widespread German pogroms was not due to any lack of desire by the *völkisch* groups before 1933. It was a tactical choice by their Nazi successors from 1933 to 1938.[58] The Summer Olympic Games in Berlin, in August 1936 (and the less heralded Winter Olympics in Garmisch-Partenkirchen in February 1936), figured in Hitler's calculated, temporary 'restraint'. Pogroms may not have immediately materialized, but Wiener was right to call attention to the agitation for economic boycotts against Jews, sporadic violence and other forms of persecution.[59]

'The antisemites,' he argues, 'focus on targeting two social classes: the workers and the military.' This was based on evidence he gathered from 1918 to 1919.[60] But Wiener underestimated how much these *völkisch* ideas had spread, even before the outbreak of the Great War, gaining popularity among rural populations, students, primary- and secondary-school teachers and students and academics at Germany's universities. It flourished in nationalist choirs, and hiking, shooting and sporting clubs. Wiener was mainly thinking about young men, in cities, approached as potential 'pogrom agitators'.[61] He was dismayed by the anonymous workers who, claiming to be Social Democrats, would 'plead poignantly in print with their colleagues to shake off their Jewish leaders and, amid fanfare, to sign up to the cause of antisemitism, that alone offers salvation'. Factory floors were flooded with 'hundreds of thousands' of such calls to embrace *völkisch* nationalism as somehow akin to the aims of social democracy.[62]

Speaking of the *völkisch* presence in the Reichswehr, the German army, Wiener had spotted one of the gravest dangers not only to Jews, but to the Weimar Republic itself. He cites, for example, 'the Educational Service of the Lettow-Vorbeck Brigade', headed by Joseph Karl (Hans) Knauer (1895–1952), which expressly advocated pogroms and public hangings of Jews.[63] Hitler himself gained invaluable contacts and experience in a similar position to Knauer,[64] which he conveniently omits in his autobiography, *Mein Kampf*. He sought to create a myth that he had risen purely as an artist, without any kind of institutional support beyond his wartime service.

Although he lays stress on workers and soldiers, Wiener nevertheless understands that the backers of *völkisch* ideology cast their nets wide, tailoring appeals to lawyers, engineers, school children, young mothers and clergy.[65] Some of these efforts yielded more fruit than others. Historian Robert Ericksen reveals that, rather than having to undergo *Gleichschaltung* – that is, to be 'coordinated' with the regime – German churches and universities were in large measure already Nazified by the time Hitler gained power in 1933.[66]

In addition to issuing a warning about impending pogroms, Wiener also undertook a series of debunking exercises in these pamphlets. 'People are keen,' he writes, 'to spread the fairy tale of monstrous Jewish wealth. The money raised on the Jewish side of this debate, however, has never matched the sums the antisemites now spend on their dark machinations.'[67] That was not the most elegant way to say that Jews had not, thus far, collectively used their financial muscle for advancing their own interests against those who threatened them.

Wiener asserted, correctly, that a sizeable portion of the German-Jewish population was not wealthy, but working and lower-middle class, including some who were impoverished. Although he highlighted German Jewry's economic diversity, Wiener refrained from mentioning that, since the 1860s, an increasing share of Jews was migrating westward from Poland, and elsewhere in Eastern Europe, into Germany. George Mosse used to quip that his mother ran a soup kitchen for newly arrived immigrant Jews in Berlin, out of the goodness of her heart – but also with the thought of speeding them on their way to America.

The most important of the German industrial concerns, the 'mammoth companies', were not owned by Jews.[68] The exception was AEG, the German general electric company, which was founded by the father of Walther Rathenau. Nor did Jews control the country's largest mining conglomerates or land-holdings.[69] Some of the *völkisch* stalwarts, Wiener notes, like Alfred Roth (1879–1948), were from the realm of 'heavy industry' management, and corporate magnates were among those bankrolling the movement.[70] 'One of the most extraordinary aspects of modern German history,' Gerald Feldman reminds us in his history of *Allianz and the German Insurance Business, 1933–1945*, 'is that so many of its greatest enterprises have managed to survive the misadventures of its political history.'[71]

This occasion of republishing Alfred Wiener's early pamphlets also may help to dismiss a widely held dichotomy (up to today), that Germany's Jews were fundamentally divided between those extolling 'the Fatherland', Germany, versus the Zionists, promoting 'the Promised Land', i.e. the colonization of their ancestral homeland of Palestine, the Land of Israel. The interpretation of Carl Schorske, in which he situates Zionism as part of a 'politics in a new key', has proven more penetrating.[72] Yet this division is still apparent in comment about

German Jews, and is expressed crudely as assimilationists versus Zionists. An underlying assumption is that Zionists sensed the dangers of antisemitism and were militant, while the assimilationists were mutely passive. Alfred Wiener's perspective, speaking as a German patriot and a proud Jew, transcends these categories. His writing complements the increasingly complex scholarly depictions and analyses of Central European Jewry.[73] Zionism is not mentioned in these pamphlets. In addition to seeing the movement as slapdash and disrespectful of Palestine's native Arabs, perhaps Wiener was put off because some of the mystical, nationalist ideas he was denouncing in the realm of German ultra-nationalism also had a place, however muted, in Zionism. (Decades later George Mosse detected that ideas akin to *völkisch* nationalism were appropriated by Jewish groups as well.)[74]

In contrast to assimilationist-versus-Zionist reductionism, Wiener depicts German Jewry as occupying every station on the country's political spectrum, including the far right (that is, before 1925).[75] This divergence dramatically played out in Bavaria, with disastrous consequences.[76] Wiener also explains why Jews generally were most at home with the Social Democrats and the centre-left, and comfortable with an 'internationalist' mindset.[77] In the former Russian Empire, it made sense for Jews to rebel against the 'oppression and darkness' inflicted on them by the Tsars.[78] The common conservative view, though, that Bolshevik leaders were mainly Jews, or acted in the 'Jewish interest', was untrue.[79] To the extent that they can even be considered a community,[80] Jews, Wiener argued, tended to be 'conservative', even if they didn't vote that way. And the fact of the matter was, he adds, that Jews were 'never… wanted in the right-wing parties'.[81] The Jewish people, Wiener asserts at the conclusion of his 1924 address, 'are not a unity, they are a multiplicity; just as colourful, as political, as econom-ically divided as the German people'.[82]

Although the Social Democrats may not have been prone to anti-Jewish violence, Wiener believed they were remiss in defending Jews, failing to ensure the solidarity they professed to uphold. Wiener and his Centralverein colleagues were not qui-escent in the face of persecution.[83] The recent research of Wolf Gruner brings to light the intensity with which the CV chal-lenged antisemites in the press and the courts, with some degree of success.[84] German Jews of the CV were bereft neither of eth-nic pride nor of Jewish consciousness. The epigraph by Gabriel Rießer (1806–63) that Wiener selected for his second pam-phlet, *German Jewry in Political, Economic and Cultural Perspective*, speaks volumes: 'If someone disputes my claim on my German fatherland, he disputes my right to my thoughts, my feelings, to the language that I speak and the air that I breathe. That is why I must defend myself against him – as against a murderer.'[85] Historian Marion Kaplan, analysing Jewish daily life once the Nazis gained power, argues that Jews experienced a 'social death' in having their very identities extinguished.[86]

Perhaps one of Alfred Wiener's more inscrutable arguments, for a twenty-first century audience, is his disavowal of 'philo-Semitism'.[87] What does this mean? Why should Wiener not want Germans to be 'Jew-loving'? Historian Lars Fischer shows that German Social Democrats routinely claimed to oppose antisemitism, while simultaneously affirming that they were not 'philo-Semitic'. This was a signal that they would not be inordinately inclined to treat Jews generously.[88] Wiener finds this more or less acceptable. In 1919, he wrote: 'We Jews wish that any one of us who harms the German people or our German fatherland be held strictly to account. Which section of the population is made up entirely of saints?'[89] Reiterating the point in 1924, Wiener said: 'The decisive issue is that we as German Jews are not better or worse than the world around us.'[90] Likewise, 'the "Jewish spirit" is not better but also not worse than the spirit of the environment in which it dwells'.[91]

This had to be clearly articulated because, in the wake of the Great War, there were, in fact, a number of Jews who engaged in large-scale scandals and swindles. These men were unfortunately conflated with those the German right vaguely denounced as the 'November criminals' who were behind the imaginary 'stab in the back'.[92] 'But it is a tremendous outrage,' Wiener added, 'to agitate irresponsibly for violence against all Jews for the failings of individuals, when the consequences are unforeseeable. Where does that leave morality, where does it leave justice, and how are we to arrive at an orderly reconstruction after the ghastly collapse of the fatherland, if these cornerstones are missing?'[93]

While this may have been heartening to his non-Jewish readership, Wiener was perhaps oblivious to how slippery the notion of 'anti-philo-Semitism' could be. To claim opposition to 'philo-Semitism' before 1939 is akin to Republicans in the United States, since the 1980s, saying that they are 'not racist' but that they are 'against affirmative action'. Being 'anti-philo-Semitic' was a German version of what was termed in America the 'gentleman's agreement' – a pledge to (quietly, if possible) exclude Jews from society's most dignified circles. But this chink in the Social Democrats' armour might have been ameliorated if not for the worldwide depression of 1929, which is beyond the purview of Wiener's writings here.

In the litany of antisemitic charges, the most personally demeaning to Alfred Wiener was the canard that German Jews had shirked their wartime duty, acted cowardly and not sacrificed for the nation to the same extent as had other Germans.[94] Wiener had put his specialized knowledge to use in the war, had himself been under fire, and nearly died from disease through wartime deprivation. Wiener defends the Jewish soldiers' honour with vigour in both addresses, without talking about himself.[95] He relates, in 1924, that the recently deceased *völkisch* publicist, Dietrich Eckart (1868–1923), had staged a 'competition' on the subject of the 'Jewish census' (*Judenzählung*, 1916) in the First World War trenches. Eckart claimed that it would be impossible to find 'a Jewish mother who had three sons on the front line for three weeks' – the proper standard, Eckart thought, of sacrifice for the nation. He would give, he pledged, a prize of 1,000 marks, 'a considerable sum at that time', if such a woman existed. Lo and behold, 'Rabbi Dr Freund from Hanover submitted a list of twenty such families', which Eckart refused to accept. He was sued, lost in court and had to pay. And in court 'Dr Freund demonstrated not only that twenty Jewish families had three sons on the front line for three weeks, he provided a list of fifty Jewish families who had up to eight sons on the front line of battle for three weeks'.[96]

Dietrich Eckart is recognized as a co-founder of the Deutsche Arbeiterpartei (German Workers' Party, DAP) in Munich, which in 1921 became the Nationalsozialistische

Deutsche Arbeiterpartei [NSDAP, National Socialist German Workers' Party] – commonly known as the Nazis.[97] 'National Socialism' in this context was not much interested in the living standards of workers, and had nothing to do with Marxism.[98] Derived in part from the writings of French antisemite Alphonse de Toussenel (1803–85), 'National Socialism' prescribed that 'Jewish wealth' must be expropriated and distributed among the nation's upright 'Aryan' peasantry.[99] The platform of the DAP vehemently opposed the ideals of the Enlightenment and liberal democracies. It espoused pan-German conquest, heightened anxieties about modern society, and promised to create a heaven on earth through putting its racial antisemitism into practice.[100] Eckart made a determined effort to befriend Adolf Hitler when he joined the small group.[101]

It was Eckart, according to George Mosse, 'who exercised the greatest influence on Adolf Hitler in the immediate postwar years'.[102] Akin to Hitler's self-image as a brilliant but misunderstood artist, whose career was blocked by Jews, Eckart saw himself as a literary genius whose talent was thwarted because of Jewish press and publishing lords. Finding few outlets for his articles, despite numerous antisemitic papers, Eckart issued his own newssheet, *Auf gut Deutsch* [*In Plain German*]. When offered for free on the street it was rarely grabbed. So Eckart 'resorted to distributing it personally to commuters on crowded trains in Munich'.[103] He was among those who captivated Hitler with visions of diabolical Jewish conspiracies, and advocated that Germany's Jews should be sealed in medieval-like ghettos. Apparently Eckart introduced Hitler to General Ludendorff, who provided the Nazis with greater access to elites and funds (and who three years later would figure prominently in the 'Beer Hall Putsch'). On that same occasion, 16 March 1920, Hitler was welcomed into 'the salon of Helen Bechstein, the wife of the piano manufacturer', and met Heinrich Claß, president of a large pan-German association, the Altdeutscher Verband.[104]

While Hitler, specifically, does not appear in these pamphlets, his exploits were certainly known to Alfred Wiener. At the time of Wiener's talk on German Jewry, on 25 January 1924, Hitler was awaiting trial, having been arrested for his lead role in the 'Beer Hall Putsch' of 9 November 1923. The party was officially banned, and replacement groups were formed during Hitler's imprisonment. In Bavaria, the Völkischer Block (National Block) was established by Alfred Rosenberg, who had supposedly been deputized by Hitler. Another organization, the Großdeutsche Volksgemeinschaft (Greater German People's Community), was founded, and pointedly refused to engage in any Weimar political process. Beyond Bavaria yet another alternate body was formed, the Deutschvölkische Freiheitspartei

(German Nationalist Freedom Party), which later called itself the Nationalsozialistische Freiheitsbewegung. Hitler did not himself have much to do with these developments.[105]

The flawed judicial proceedings to try the perpetrators of the Beer Hall Putsch commenced on 26 February 1924. A sympathetic judge allowed Hitler to give long, uninterrupted speeches that inflated his reputation. The *völkisch* press reported his grandstanding as 'news'. Hitler's conditions in the Landsberg prison were also unusually comfortable.[106] He used the time to dictate *Mein Kampf*. During his brief captivity (serving less than a year of a five-year term), Hitler decided that his earlier attempt to gain state power by force should not be repeated. He self-consciously sought to distance himself from the *völkisch* figures among whom he had been schooled and from whose ranks he had emerged. He even chastised them, including his friend Eckart, 'for lacking "all political sense"'.[107] Hitler thought, instead, to exercise patience, planning to further cultivate relationships with the high and mighty, and use the instruments of democracy to infiltrate and overturn the Weimar Republic. Wiener was completely reasonable in leaving Hitler out of the picture. Hitler was a fantasist and a compulsive liar, and often derided for his atrocious German that would estrange him from the respectable political arena. This view is probably best illustrated in Lion Feuchtwanger's prescient novel,

The Oppermanns, of 1933.[108] And Hitler was, after all, one of
the most ardent believers in the ludicrous *völkisch* hotchpotch,
particularly its racialized mysticism, with the notion that Jews
were evil incarnate at its core.[109] Although the company he
kept had raised alarm bells, one is hard-pressed to find anyone outside of the *völkisch* circles, before 1924, who entertained
the possibility that Adolf Hitler would upend the Weimar
Republic.

The 'pogrom militia' about which Alfred Wiener forewarned
in 1919 may be seen as materializing, after 1933, with the central organs of terror in the Third Reich: the SA and the SS, the
latter under Heinrich Himmler (1900–45). Himmler, too, was
a fervent *völkist*. Instead of pogroms, a chief vehicle for perse-
cuting – and later systematically murdering – Jews and other
opponents would be the concentration camp.[110] The Nazis did,
however, use pogroms in Eastern Europe during the Second
World War to enable the 'actions' of the *Einsatzgruppen* which
left over a million Jews dead by shooting.

For Alfred Wiener, it was reasonable to think that the
Weimar Republic might survive into the indefinite future,
especially as the further restructuring of its Versailles-imposed
debt helped make reparations payments manageable. But in
1929 the worldwide depression, sparked in the United States,

hit the German economy. The phantoms surrounding the Central Powers' defeat in the Great War, and Weimar's tumultuous birth pangs, provided incendiary political capital in the early 1930s. The spectre of Communism also enhanced the Nazis' standing immeasurably. Hitler's path to power, and the genocide of European Jewry, were the results of improvisation and catastrophic coincidences along a grotesquely twisted road.[111] National Socialism was far from categorically rigid, showing particular flexibility in areas such as the law (largely conservative even in Weimar times), medical research and environmental policy.[112] But if there was little agreement among Germans, after 1933, over what the Nazis stood *for*, everyone knew that the regime was dead set *against* the Jews.[113] *Völkisch* nationalists had, however, neither been predetermined, since 1919, to capture Germany's leadership, nor to perpetrate the annihilation, during wartime, of two thirds of European Jewry. Hitler, Himmler and their accomplices turned *völkisch* lies and pseudo-intellectual garbage into a hell on earth. The insights of Alfred Wiener about *völkisch* nationalism and the actual lives of German Jews, from 1919 and 1924, are among the more poignant contemporary signposts that history and the Wiener Holocaust Library have bequeathed to later generations.

Dedicated to Andy Rabinbach.

My thanks to Christine Schmidt, Toby Simpson and

Sigrid Rausing for their extremely helpful assistance.

Notes

1 As Ben Barkow argued and demonstrated in his seminal *Alfred Wiener and the Making of the Holocaust Library* (London and Portland, OR: Valentine Mitchell, 1997), the person, Alfred Wiener, is inextricable from the entity he created.

2 See Nils H. Roemer, *Jewish Scholarship and Culture in Nineteenth-Century Germany: Between History and Faith* (Madison, WI: University of Wisconsin Press, 2005).

3 Barkow, *Alfred Wiener*, p. 6.

4 I wish to thank Maryam Ismail for providing this important insight; personal communication with the author, 16 June 2020.

5 Alfred Wiener, *Kritische Reise durch Palästina: mit 13 Karten und Zeichnungen* (Berlin: Philo Verlag, 1927, 1928); Alfred Wiener, *Juden und Araber in Palästina: zur Erkenntnis der jüngsten Vorgänge* (Berlin: Philo Verlag, 1929); Barkow, *Alfred Wiener*, pp. 20–27.

6 Barkow, *Alfred Wiener*, pp. 7–8.

7 Michael Berkowitz, *Zionist Culture and West European Jewry before the First World War* (Cambridge: Cambridge University Press, 1993), pp. 113 and 158; Barkow, *Alfred Wiener*, pp. 7–8. The Hilfsverein was similar, in outlook, to the French Alliance Israélite Universelle; see Aron Rodrigue, *Images of Sephardi and Eastern Jewries in Transition: The Teachers of the Alliance Israélite Universelle, 1860–1939* (Seattle: WA, University of Washington Press, 1993).

8 Barkow, *Alfred Wiener*, p. 8.

9 Stefan Lorant, *SIEG HEIL! (HAIL TO VICTORY): An Illustrated History of Germany from Bismarck to Hitler* (New York: W.W. Norton & Company, 1974), p. 66.

10 Sebastian Haffner, *Defying Hitler: A Memoir*, tr. Oliver Pretzel (London: Weidenfeld & Nicolson, 2002), p. 18, note.

11 Paul Mendes-Flohr, *Martin Buber: A Life of Faith and Dissent* (New Haven, CT and London: Yale University Press, 2019), p. 128.

12 David Biale, *Gershom Scholem: Master of the Kabbalah* (New Haven, CT and London: Yale University Press, 2018), p. 14; Adi Gordon, *Toward Nationalism's End: An Intellectual Biography of Hans Kohn* (Waltham, MA: Brandeis University Press, 2017), p. 82; see also Michael Löwy, *Redemption & Utopia: Jewish Libertarian Thought in Central Europe: A Study in Elective Affinity*, tr. Hope Heaney (Stanford, CA: Stanford University Press, 1992). Scholem and Buber were leading advocates for shared binational rights of Jews and Arabs in Palestine, and Kohn eventually rejected Zionism altogether, becoming a vociferous critic of the movement over this issue.

13 Jack Jacobs, *The Frankfurt School, Jewish Lives, and Antisemitism* (New York: Cambridge University Press, 2014).

14 Milan Hauner, *Hitler: A Chronology of His Life and Time*, 2nd rev. edn (Houndmills, Basingstoke and New York: Palgrave Macmillan, 2008), p. 29.

15 See George S. Vascik and Mark R. Sadler (eds), *The Stab-in-the-Back Myth and the Fall of the Weimar Republic: A History in Documents and Visual Sources* (London: Bloomsbury Academic, 2016).

16 Brendan Simms, *Hitler: A Global Biography* (New York: Basic Books, 2019).

17 'Dr Alfred Wiener', Sourasky Central Library, Tel Aviv University, at en-cenlib.m.tau.ac.il/Wiener/Alfred-Wiener [accessed 15 June 2020]. The article credits Barkow, *Alfred Wiener*.

18 In addition to Barkow's *Alfred Wiener*, a number of websites have appropriated information from the entry 'Wiener, Alfred' from Robert Wistrich, *Who's Who in Nazi Germany* (London: Weidenfeld and Nicolson, 1982), pp. 339–40.

19 Alfred Wiener, *The Fatherland and the Jews*, present volume, pp. 81–2, 84–6 and 86–9.

20 Charges of 'ritual murder', the absurd allegation of Jews killing Christians for religious purposes, were among those spread in 'leaflets and flyers' in the millions, *Fatherland*, pp. 48–9, 52, 56 and 64–6.

21 *Fatherland*, pp. 55–6.

22 *Fatherland*, p. 69.

23 *Fatherland*, pp. 49–50.

24 *Fatherland*, pp. 54–5.

25 *Fatherland*, pp. 47–8.

26 *Fatherland*, pp. 62–3.

27 *Fatherland*, pp. 118–19.

28 *Fatherland*, pp. 54–5.

29 *Fatherland*, p. 83.

30 *Fatherland*, pp. 50–51.

31 Steven E. Aschheim, *Brothers and Strangers: The East European Jew in German and German Jewish Consciousness 1800–1923* (Madison, WI: University of Wisconsin Press, 1982), p. 233.

32 *Fatherland*, pp. 55–7.

33 *Fatherland*, pp. 81–2. In the second of the pamphlets, Wiener attempts to quote mainly from non-Jews in refuting the anti-semitic charges.

34 Hauner, *Hitler Chronology*, entry for 21 November 1922, p. 37.

35 *Fatherland*, pp. 48–9, 50–51 and 52–3.

36 Among those who went bankrupt from the Central Powers losing the war were the children of Theodor Herzl (1860–1904), the founder of the Zionist movement. Their trust fund had been invested in Austrian war bonds, which became worthless.

37 *Fatherland*, pp. 113–14; see Philipp Nielsen, *Between Heimat and Hatred: Jews and the Right in Germany, 1871–1935* (New York: Oxford University Press, 2019).

38 Rathenau is mentioned only in passing in *Fatherland*, p. 112.

39 Haffner, *Defying Hitler*, pp. 37 and 36–41. See also Peter Loewenberg, 'Walther Rathenau and German society' (PhD dissertation, University of California, 1966), which is difficult to access but unsurpassed; see also James Joll, *Intellectuals in Politics: Three Biographical Essays* (London: Weidenfeld & Nicolson, 1960); Shulamit Volkov, *Walther Rathenau: The Life of Weimar's Fallen Statesman* (New Haven, CT: Yale University Press, 2012).

40 Haffner, *Defying Hitler*, p. 36.

41 Haffner, *Defying Hitler*, p. 38. Perhaps the most moving piece of

speculative writing on the course of modern history is Michael
Brenner's essay imagining what 'might have' happened had
Rathenau not been assassinated; see Michael Brenner, 'What
if the Weimar Republic had survived? A chapter from Walther
Rathenau's memoir', in *What Ifs of Jewish History: From Abraham
to Zionism*, ed. Gavriel Rosenfeld (New York and Cambridge:
Cambridge University Press, 2016), pp. 259–74.

42 Gordon A. Craig, *The Germans* (New York: G. P. Putnam's Sons,
    1982), p. 143.

43 Translated differently, the *Deutscher Schutz- und Trutzbund* is
    mentioned in *Fatherland*, p. 48.

44 Hauner, *Hitler Chronology*, p. 25.

45 Hauner, *Hitler Chronology*, p. 21.

46 Siegfried Kracauer, *From Caligari to Hitler: A Psychological History
    of the German Film* (Princeton, NJ: Princeton University Press,
    1966), p. 43; [Spartacus Manifesto], first published as 'Richtlinien
    für die Arbeiter- und Soldatenräte Deutschlands' in *Die rote Fahne*
    (26 November 1918), in *Weimar Republic Sourcebook*, pp. 37–8.

47 George L. Mosse, *Toward the Final Solution: A History of European
    Racism* (Madison, WI: University of Wisconsin Press, 1985),
    p. 183.

48 *Fatherland*, p. 55.

49 Fritz Stern, *The Politics of Cultural Despair: A Study in the Rise of
    the Germanic Ideology* (Berkeley: University of California Press,
    1963 [c.1961]); George L. Mosse, *The Crisis of German Ideology:
    Intellectual Origins of the Third Reich* (New York: Grosset &
    Dunlap, 1964).

50 Moshe Zimmermann, 'Mosse and German Historiography',
    in *George L. Mosse: On the Occasion of His Retirement, 17.6.85*
    (Jerusalem: The Koebner Chair of German History, The
    Hebrew University of Jerusalem, 1986), pp. xiv–xxi.

51 George Mosse acknowledges 'the research for this book took me
    to three continents, a reflection of the dispersal of Volkish mate-
    rials. In Germany, the Institut für Zeitgeschichte in Munich and
    the Bayerische Staatsbibliothek... the archives of the German
    Youth Movement at Burg Ludwigstein... the Bundesarchiv
    in Koblenz... In Jerusalem, both the Library of the Hebrew
    University and the Jewish National Archives... [in the United

States] the Hoover Institution on War, Revolution and Peace
[and] the University of Wisconsin library…', *The Crisis of German
Ideology*, p. v.

52 Barkow, *Alfred Wiener*, p. 146.

53 Saul Friedländer, *Nazi Germany and the Jews* (New York:
HarperCollins, 1997); Christian Wiese and Paul Betts (eds),
*Years of Persecution, Years of Extermination: Saul Friedländer and the
Future of Holocaust Studies* (London and New York: Continuum,
2010), pp. 115–210.

54 Emily J. Levine, *Dreamland of Humanists: Warburg, Cassirer,
Panofsky, and the Hamburg School* (Chicago, IL: University of
Chicago Press, 2013).

55 John Klier, *Russians, Jews and the Pogroms of 1881–1882* (Cambridge
and New York: Cambridge University Press, 2011); Eugene
M. Avrutin and Harriet Murav (eds), *Jews in the East European
Borderlands: Essays in Honor of John D. Klier* (Boston, MA,
Academic Studies Press, 2012).

56 Alan E. Steinweis, *Kristallnacht 1938* (Cambridge, MA: Belknap
Press of the Harvard University Press, 2009); Ruth Levitt (ed.),
Pogrom: November 1938: Testimonies from Kristallnacht (London:
Souvenir Press, published in association with The Wiener
Library for the Study of the Holocaust and Genocide, 2015).

57 François Guesnet and Uli Baumann, 'Kristallnacht-Pogrom-
Terror. A Terminological Reflection', in *New Perspectives on
Kristallnacht after 80 Years: The Nazi Pogrom in Global Comparison*,
ed. Wolf Gruner and Steven Ross (Lafayette, IN: Purdue
University Press, 2020), forthcoming.

58 *Fatherland*, pp. 57–8.

59 *Fatherland*, pp. 56–7.

60 Brian E. Crim, *Antisemitism in the German Military Community
and the Jewish Response* (Lanham, MD: Lexington, 2014).

61 *Fatherland*, p. 52.

62 *Fatherland*, pp. 52–4.

63 *Fatherland*, pp. 54–5.

64 This was well known; see '*The Brown Book*. The road to power'
[1933], in *The Third Reich Sourcebook*, ed. Anson Rabinbach
and Sander L. Gilman (Berkeley and Los Angeles, and London:
University of California Press, 2013), p. 844.

65 *Fatherland*, pp. 55–7.

66 Robert P. Ericksen, *Complicity in the Holocaust: Churches and Universities in Nazi Germany* (New York, Cambridge University Press, 2012).

67 *Fatherland*, p. 47.

68 *Fatherland*, pp. 50–51, 99–100, 108–111.

69 *Fatherland*, pp. 111–12.

70 *Fatherland*, pp. 48–9.

71 Gerald D. Feldman, *Allianz and the German Insurance Business, 1933–1945* (New York, Cambridge University Press, 2001), p. 1.

72 Jehuda Reinharz, *Fatherland or Promised Land: The Dilemma of the German Jew, 1893–1914* (Ann Arbor, MI: University of Michigan Press, 1975). Although Reinharz's study ends with the Great War, the stark divisions he describes were more complex even then; see Carl E. Schorske, 'Politics in a New Key: An Austrian Triptych', *The Journal of Modern History*, 39 (December 1967), pp. 343–86, also in Schorske's classic, *Fin-de-Siècle Vienna: Politics and Culture* (New York: Vintage, 1981), pp. 116–180.

73 See especially Marion A. Kaplan, *The Making of the Jewish Middle Class: Women, Family, and Identity in Imperial Germany* (New York and Oxford: Oxford University Press, 1991); Michael Brenner, *The Renaissance of Jewish Culture in Weimar Germany* (New Haven, CT: Yale University Press, 1996); John M. Efron, *German Jewry and the Allure of the Sephardic* (Princeton, NJ: Princeton University Press, 2016); Sharon Gillerman, *Germans into Jews: Remaking the Jewish Social Body in the Weimar Republic* (Stanford, CA: Stanford University Press, 2009); Paul Lerner, *The Consuming Temple: Jews, Department Stores, and the Consumer Revolution in Germany, 1880–1940* (Ithaca, NY: Cornell University Press, 2015); Jay Howard Geller, *The Scholems: A Story of the German-Jewish Bourgeoisie from Emancipation to Destruction* (Ithaca, NY: Cornell University Press, 2019).

74 George L. Mosse, 'The influence of the Völkisch idea on German Jewry', in *Studies of the Leo Baeck Institute* (New York: Frederik Unger, 1967), pp. 81–115; also in Mosse, *Germans and Jews: The Right, the Left, and the Search for a 'Third Force' in Pre-Nazi Germany* (New York: Howard Fertig, 1960).

75 *Fatherland*, pp. 91–4 and 112–13.

76 Michael Brenner, *Der lange Schatten der Revolution. Juden und Antisemiten in Hitlers München 1918–1923* (Berlin: Jüdischer Verlag im Suhrkamp Verlag, 2019).

77 *Fatherland*, pp. 91–4 and 93–6.

78 *Fatherland*, pp. 94–6.

79 *Fatherland*, pp. 95–8.

80 *Fatherland*, pp. 98–9.

81 *Fatherland*, p. 91.

82 *Fatherland*, pp. 118–19.

83 Formally translated as 'the Central Association of German Citizens of Jewish Faith'; *Fatherland*, p. 79.

84 Wolf Gruner, 'Indifference, participation, protest? Responses to the persecution of the Jews as revealed in Berlin police logs and trial records 1933–1945', in *The Germans and the Persecution of the Jews*, ed. Wolf Gruner (New York: Berghahn, 2015), pp. 59–83; Wolf Gruner and Thomas Pegelow Kaplan (eds), *Resisting Persecution: Jews and Their Petitions during the Holocaust* (New York: Berghahn, 2019).

85 *Fatherland*, p. 77.

86 Marion A. Kaplan, *Between Dignity and Despair: Jewish Life in Nazi Germany* (New York: Oxford University Press, 1998).

87 *Fatherland*, pp. 88–9 and 119.

88 Lars Fischer, *The Socialist Response to Antisemitism in Imperial Germany* (Cambridge: Cambridge University Press, 2007).

89 *Fatherland*, pp. 67–9.

90 *Fatherland*, p. 108.

91 *Fatherland*, pp. 118–19.

92 Michael Berkowitz, *The Crime of My Very Existence: Nazism and the Myth of Jewish Criminality* (Berkeley and Los Angeles: University of California Press, 2007), pp. 15, 18, 23 and 119.

93 *Fatherland*, pp. 67–9.

94 On the 'Jew count of 1916' see Derek J. Penslar, *Jews and the Military: A History* (Princeton, NJ, and Oxford: Princeton University Press, 2013), p. 173.

95 *Fatherland*, pp. 47–9, 67–9 and 102–107.

96 *Fatherland*, pp. 104–5.

97 'The Program of the National-Socialist (Nazi) German Workers' Party', in *Documents on the Holocaust*, ed. Yitzhak Arad, Israel Gutman and Abraham Margaliot, tr. Lea Ben Dor (Lincoln: University of Nebraska Press and Jerusalem: Yad Vashem, 1999), pp. 15–18.

98 Mosse, *Toward the Final Solution*, pp. 152–4; see also Hauner, *Hitler Chronology*, entry for 11 November 1922, p. 36.

99 Mosse, *Toward the Final Solution*, pp. 152–4.

100 Anson Rabinbach and Sander L. Gilman (eds), *The Third Reich Sourcebook* (Berkeley and Los Angeles, and London: University of California Press, 2013), p. 4.

101 Mosse, *Crisis of German Ideology*, p. 297.

102 Mosse, *Crisis of German Ideology*, p. 26.

103 Mosse, *Crisis of German Ideology*, p. 297.

104 Hauner, *Hitler Chronology*, p. 21.

105 Hauner, *Hitler Chronology*, p. 46.

106 Jan Friedmann, 'Flowers for the Führer in Landsberg Prison. New historical documents show that Adolf Hitler wanted for nothing during his short incarceration at Landsberg Prison in 1924. He was able to hold court and maintain his political contacts – all with the consent of the prison management', *Der Spiegel*, 23 June 2010, spiegel.de/international/germany/adolf-hitler-s-time-in-jail-flowers-for-the-fuehrer-in-landsberg-prison-a-702159.html [accessed 17 May 2020].

107 Mosse, *Toward the Final Solution*, p. 206.

108 Lion Feuchtwanger, *The Oppermans*, translated by James Cleugh (New York: Carroll & Graf, Inc. 2001).

109 Mosse, *Toward the Final Solution*, pp. 205–6.

110 Kim Wünschmann, *Before Auschwitz: Jewish Prisoners in the Prewar Concentration Camps* (Cambridge, MA and London: Harvard University Press, 2015).

111 Karl A. Schleunes, *The Twisted Road to Auschwitz: Nazi Policy toward German Jews, 1933–1939* (Urbana, IL, University of Illinois Press, 1970); David Cesarani, *Final Solution: The Fate of the Jews, 1933–1949* (London: Macmillan, 2016); Christopher Browning, *The Origins of the Final Solution: The Evolution of Nazi Jewish Policy, September 1939–March 1942* (Lincoln: University of Nebraska Press and Jerusalem: Yad Vashem, 2004).

112 Anson Rabinbach and Sander L. Gilman (eds.), *The Third Reich Sourcebook* (Berkeley and Los Angeles, and London: University of California Press, 2013), p. 109; see also Robert N. Proctor, *The Nazi War on Cancer* (Princeton, NJ: Princeton University Press, 1999) and Raymond H. Dominick III, *The Environmental Movement in Germany: Prophets and Pioneers* (Bloomington, IN: Indiana University Press, 1992).

113 Rabinbach and Gilman, *The Third Reich Sourcebook*, p. 109.

Alfred Wiener

Prelude to Pogroms?

FACTS FOR THOUGHTFUL PEOPLE.

1919

Verlag 'Gabriel Rießer'
Berlin SW 68 Lindenstr. 13[1]

A MIGHTY ANTISEMITIC storm has broken over us, a storm that has not come about according to the laws of physics, but rather by means of unlimited funds in the hands of skilfully led organizations, which have stimulated and promoted it and are zealously seeking to further it. People are keen to spread the fairy tale of monstrous Jewish wealth. The money raised on the Jewish side of this debate, however, has never matched the sums the antisemites now spend on their dark machinations. Dark machinations! It may be that our 'decent antisemites' disdain to solve the Jewish problem with shotguns and cudgels, but what does that matter to the 'men of action' who state more or less openly in leaflets – and quite fearlessly at secret meetings – that they envy the Poles and Romanians their pogroms, and who work systematically to imitate them in our dear fatherland? This is why we should describe the antisemitic rabble-rousing of our day as agitation for pogroms.

I   *The Authors of the Agitation*

The breeding ground of these poisonous leaflets is the Committee for Public Enlightenment [Ausschuss für Volksaufklärung] in Berlin W9, Köthener Straße 45, which was launched with the well-known red leaflet *The End of Militarism – The Beginning of Jewish Rule*. It has since produced more than twenty different leaflets and, in addition, has organized frequent meetings to which 'Jews are not admitted', at which it 'enlightens' its followers in the most vile tones. Its valiant helpers are the German-*Völkisch*[2] League [Deutsch-völkische Bund] in Hamburg 6, the Community for German Renewal [Deutsche Erneuerungsgemeinde] in Leipzig, the Reich Hammer League [Reichshammerbund] in Hamburg 36 and – recently established and among the most active – the German Protection and Defiance League [Deutscher Schutz- und Trutzbund]. This is now also located in Hamburg, and its executive director, the former captain Alfred Roth, comes from the circle of Westphalian heavy industry.[3] These associations, with a few others, have united to form a working group with Alfred Roth at its head. Together they are flooding Germany with leaflets, pamphlets, handbills and stickers. In addition,

48

antisemitic leaflets of the most terrible character have been distributed by the 'Director of Forestry' Max Beyer, of Berlin Wilmersdorf, Günzelstraße 36; the businessman Fellechner, Berlin Wilmersdorf, Parezer Straße 10, the farmer Friedrich Sähring from Saugarten in the March of Brandenburg, and the commercial judge (not sitting) Robert Christ.

Apart from the leagues, a number of daily newspapers work diligently to see that the antisemitic seed is widely sown and nurtured. Anyone who follows these daily newspapers with a professional interest gains the strong impression that some central source has put out the word to agitate vigorously against the Jews. Taking the lead is the *Deutsche Zeitung*, which has always been on first-name terms with antisemitism – who doesn't know Friedrich Lange? – and which now rails unscrupulously and obscenely against the Jews to stoke up pogroms.[4] Close on its dubious heels is the *Deutsche Tageszeitung*, the worthy organ of the League of Farmers, whose editorial office has a close relationship with the Reich Hammer League. In it the grim Pan-German Count Reventlow – married to a French woman – and our 'old friends' Richard Nordhausen and Philipp Stauff work more assiduously than ever to throttle the Jews, the former in the political section and the latter in the feature pages.[5] We must also not forget the *Tägliche Rundschau*, and provincial newspapers such as the *Hallesche Zeitung* and the Stuttgart *Süddeutsche Zeitung*, which ensure that no part of the Reich misses out on the 'antisemitic enlightenment'.

In Berlin, a new antisemitic weekly paper, the *Deutsche Wochenblatt*, has emerged into the dull light of this poor world. The editor is Richard Kunze, formerly general secretary of the Conservative Party, who plays first fiddle at the meetings of the Pogrom-Antisemitic Committee for Public Enlightenment.[6] Meanwhile, his paper – well, dear Wilhelm Bruhn, you old 'Fighter for the Truth', forgive us everything we heaped on your head![7] Truly, your 'Truth' is nobly written in comparison to the 'lovely' tone taken by the *Deutsche Wochenblatt* and the incitements in almost every one of its issues. The *Münchner Beobachter* is similar, although at least it believes that it is not only the Jewish spirit, but also the Jesuit one, that rules Germany now.

It is regrettable that such a widely distributed Catholic weekly as the *Leo* of Paderborn goes along with this. It does not shy away from dishing up in almost every issue stale antisemitic lies that have been disproved a hundred times. Even *Germania*, the leading organ of the Centre

Party, completely fails to arrive at a fair assessment in its essay about Jews and Spartacists (morning edition of 1 July).[8]

We must not overlook 'scientific elucidation'. Its pioneer is the monthly *Deutschlands Erneuerung*, edited by Privy Councillor G. von Below, H. St. Chamberlain, H. Claß, Prof. R. Geyer-Wien, Privy Councillor M. von Gruber, Privy Councillor Prof. Dr Dietr. Schäfer, Dr G.W. Schiele, Chairman of the Regional Council v. Schwerin, Privy Councillor R. Seeberg.[9] It was published in Munich by J.F. Lehmann, a committee member of the German Protection and Defiance League, alongside the *Münchner Medizinische Wochenschrift* and well-known medical handbooks.[10] The most salacious essays from it are distributed widely in pamphlets, particularly Liek's sorry effort 'The Role of the Jews in Germany's Decline'.[11] This has been brilliantly refuted by Georg Davidsohn (*Im Deutschen Reich*, May issue, 1919, page 196), but the pamphlet still shines out in bright red from many booksellers' windows, and is touted enthusiastically in Berlin's streets.[12] To present the host of other antisemitic pamphlets of recent months even briefly would require an essay dedicated to nothing else.

II   *The Activities of the Agitators*

The antisemites focus on targeting two social classes: the workers and the military. And from their viewpoint, this is logical. For, as long as the pogrom agitators fail to take in the mighty army of workers in Germany, as long as the overwhelming majority of them do not salute the reactionary flag, the antisemitic efforts will find no ground in which to take root. And naturally, the agitators must pay close attention to the military. In pogroms one needs soldiers who will participate, or at least stand by without intervening.

The need for (and the advantages of) antisemitism is promoted in numerous leaflets of all colours, with and without illustrations. Yes, some who claim to be Social Democrats, but shamefully neglect to give their names, plead poignantly in print with their colleagues to shake off their Jewish leaders and, amid fanfare, to sign up to the cause of antisemitism, that alone offers salvation. Hundreds of thousands of these leaflets have been distributed, and in recent months have been sent in the post to the workers' councils in thousands of factories. Aside from this, in large factories, antisemites in workers' clothing are active, coming down hard on their colleagues. Paid agitators are travelling around the Reich, currying favour with those who are respected among the workers (those in workers' councils, etc.) and by these means spreading their poison.

And then the military. Of course, the Minister of Defence has prohibited any party-political agitation in the barracks. What do the antisemites care about that! Are there not officers who think antisemitism is so self-evident to the nobility that it's no different from wearing a monocle or speaking with the nasal drawl of the guards! And such gentlemen do not shy away from smoothing the path for these filthy leaflets in the course of their duties. It is particularly bad among the Border Defence Force East, regarding which we have heard a number of cases.[13] Still more officers make inflammatory speeches of the worst sort to their subordinates (instances from the firing range in Gruppe, near Graudenz, Frankfurt a. M.). Others do not think it necessary to remove pogrom posters from their barracks. Ten posters were proudly displayed in the barracks of the 116th in Giessen – where the well-known Jew-baiter and 'war hero' Professor Werner-Bußbach held a huge rabble-rousing meeting, as he did in Frankfurt and Marburg.[14] One of the posters showed a gallows and below it the words 'This is how you do it', and another the slogan 'Throw them into the Red Sea!'.

The crowning glory, however, is that Herr Joseph Knauer, formerly chief executive of the German-*Völkisch* League of Berlin-Schöneberg, one of the most shameless apostles of pogroms, serves in the Educational Service of the Lettow-Vorbeck Brigade.[15] His 'education' is all of the same kind. So much so, that at a meeting of representatives on 10 July of this year a Christian sergeant lashed out against Knauer's bloodthirsty hate speech.

Aside from the workers and soldiers, skilled workers are to be recruited into the antisemitic army. Leaflets are sent systematically to the homes of skilled workers in city after city. They are sent by the German-*Völkisch* bookshop of Frau Warthemann (Berlin W66, Mauerstr. 91), which is an active associate of the German-*Völkisch* League's and the Committee for Public Enlightenment. These unexpected communications are prefaced with seemingly mild words: 'Your address was given to me by someone close to the Federation of Skilled Manual Workers...'

The 'enlightenment' of teachers and clergy has also been undertaken enthusiastically. A special Headquarters for Enlightenment [Hauptstelle für Aufklärung] (Berlin SW11, Bernburger Str. 19 II, which since 20 May has been located at Berlin W9, Köthener Str. 45 III[16]), chaired by E. Foerster, has distributed 200,000 copies of a pamphlet, *On the Poisoning of the German People*, to teachers and clergy; with an introduction by a certain Dr Hoffmann (?) [*sic*]. Accompanying it is a vile flyer, presumably the intellectual property of Herr E. Foerster.

Aside from the teachers, we must not forget the pupils. Dr Dinter's *Rays of Light From the Talmud*, the work of an 'expert' who does not know a word of Hebrew, let alone Aramaic, is intended to enlighten schoolchildren (for example in Frankfurt a. M.) about Jewish writings.[17] In numerous locations (Berlin, Breslau, Kolberg among others), student associations are producing propaganda inciting violent antisemitism.[18]

German-*völkisch* lawyers and engineers have formed special unions and are spinning their webs more or less silently. German-*völkisch* Women's Unions want to make schools free of Jewish children.

The great public who do not belong to any of these groups do not escape 'education'. Individuals are paid to speak on the streets, in the trams, the trains and the elevated railway – not only in Berlin – to stir things up. When they are not being observed they speak quite openly about the desirability of plundering Jewish businesses, of murder and manslaughter.

Yes, even returning prisoners of war are met by

contingents of paid agitators, presumably as living proof of the unifying spirit of reconciliation that runs through all national comrades in this time of our fatherland's greatest need.

Some are also arming themselves economically against the Jews – and against the consumer associations. If in the past (and still today) 'Don't buy from Jews' stickers were pasted on shop windows and doors, now a General Business Federation has been formed in Magdeburg, 'a refuge for small German businesses (smallholders, merchants, consumers) from extortionate international capitalism; a protection against subversive powers (department stores, consumer associations)'. Even in its second provisional price list the Federation begs pardon for the fact that its goods are offered at prices that 'make a mockery of any calculation'.[19]

III   *The Incitements to Pogroms*

It is worthwhile to set out what mean-spirited curses, what boundless libels are contained in the hundreds of leaflets circulating in the Reich in print runs of millions. That the Jewish scriptures should be falsified in the most shameless way, that passages from works on religious laws should be hacked out of context in a completely dishonest manner, has been considered good practice by our gentlemen antisemites through the ages. In a sign of the times, we Jews are once again being burdened with the accusation of ritual murder for the purpose of manufacturing goat sausages.[20] Forgeries that were exposed decades ago, such as the notorious speech of the 'Chief Rabbi of the Kabbalah (!)' are distributed among the people in huge numbers. The leaflets in which we are drawn as animal-like lechers are disgusting. One such, purporting to come from a Greater German Protection and Defiance League for Women, but in fact originating from our dear Committee for Public Enlightenment, has been publicly distributed.[21] Another one, little known, from the same source, warns against 'sexual intercourse with Jews and other roundheads'[22] and deals so thoroughly with the anatomy of the female body below the waist that one is repelled and ashamed at such a public display. Such leaflets do not 'enlighten' anyone, but incite violence, and at this time, when, for many, human life is not worth a straw, the distance between incitement and action is a hair's breadth.

But our pogrom agitators are quite explicit about what they want to do and fear neither Hell nor the Devil.

In the weekly *Der Deutsche Volksrat*, published in Leipzig by Dr Heinrich Pudor, there is a regular feature entitled 'The Pogrom Movement' (for example, No. 13 of 24 January, No. 14 of 1 February, No. 18 of 12 March among others).[23] In this same publication (No. 21/22 of 5 April) we read the statement: 'And so it continues: the German people prefers to let itself be struck dead rather than to strike the Jews dead.' On 19 April Pudor wrote in a leading article, 'Jewish Plague': 'The mass meetings in Berlin… brought to expression an enthusiasm for the fatherland such as we have long wished for. However, striking at the guilty was entirely forgotten about.' Further on: '… we will never again achieve an orderly state of affairs in any sphere until we have dealt with the Jewish plague'. The German Protection and Defiance League has placed announcements in various German newspapers and in numerous leaflets: 'Take Jews into protective custody – then peace will reign in the land!' A flyer signed by Friedrich Sähring of Saugarten (March of Brandenburg) threatens the Jews: 'We will impale you on pitchforks.'[24] In the leaflet mentioned above from the Greater German Protection and Defiance League for Women, in reality the Committee for Public Enlightenment, we read: 'We (German women) will prove ourselves worthy of our

Germanic female ancestors who followed their men into the heat of battle, and like our immortal forebears we will ourselves take up weapons. Then woe to you cowards, woe to you lechers.' And in the infamous 'Ritual Murder' flyer of the Committee for Public Enlightenment is stated: 'Annihilate and kill all those who stand against the divine order. It is high time! Away with the criminals!'[25] This refers only to the Jews, even if the gentlemen editors, lacking all 'Germanic courage', now dispute this. A little later in the same leaflet: 'Unite and commit yourselves to decisive action!' Then: 'Up, national comrades! To action! Defend yourselves!' The German-*Völkisch* League in Berlin-Schöneberg, which shares the personnel of the Committee for Public Enlightenment, has adopted an historical approach. It cites the fabricated prophecy from the Lehnin monastery: 'Then shall Juda reach its hand for the crown and be everywhere eradicated!'[26] And it comments: 'You, people of Israel, take heed! The last part of the Lehnin prophecy may yet be fulfilled if you set out to challenge your destiny. Take heed!'

The 'Director of Forestry', Max Beyer in Berlin-Wilmersdorf, honorary member of the German-*Völkisch* League, writes quite directly: 'You have it from the mouths of the Jews themselves that they, together with a handful of persons with no honour, have created these circumstances for us. That is no more and no less than high treason to the highest degree and deserves death.' It goes on: 'We will shortly free ourselves, completely and mercilessly, from these bloodsuckers, the Jews.' Herr Fellechner, not unknown in Berlin-Wilmersdorf, wrote to the citizens of Danzig: 'If they mean to place you under Jewish rule and communal power, you must demonstrate… and if necessary, come together, resolute and strong, and fight the Jews with everything you have; for they are killing you by setting you against one another and stirring you up to fight…'

The anonymous author of a picture postcard, which originates in Czechoslovakia and is being distributed in thousands of copies around Germany, is coarsely plain. The anonymous hero unworthily mixes together passages from the scriptures and then concludes: 'Massacres of Jews must come to pass, so that they – the prophets and murderers of God – feel in their own flesh that the Mosaic prophecies are true.'

IV   *The Establishment and the Arming of the Pogrom Militia*

Hand in hand with this incitement to pogroms is the preparation of a pogrom militia by the antisemites. A secret meeting of the Committee for Public Enlightenment took place on 21 February 1919 at the 'Rheingold' in Berlin at which, among other things, the senior civil servant Ernst Grosse and Lieutenant von Arnim demanded energetic action against the Jews. A member of the organizing committee then declared to the eagerly attentive audience that according to a detailed report, the Ministry of War has sanctioned the Committee for Public Enlightenment to set up a recruitment office for volunteers. He added that, incidentally, the Minister of War was not aware that only volunteers who are committed antisemites would be recruited. This announcement unleashed frantic jubilation and those present discussed in excited groups the possibility that this could be a way to create a public weapon against the Jews. Loud cries such as 'A militia against the Jews' went up.

The German People's Union in Berlin-Schöneberg – bosom friend of the Committee for Public Enlightenment – first tried to assemble the pogrom militia under the guise of recruiting for the Border Defence Force East. As this apparently did not achieve the desired result, a poster appeared in the building of the former Royal Library, now part of Berlin University, which was then also distributed widely as a flyer. It stated: 'Volunteers from all corps... who are of Aryan-Germanic descent and who value the opportunity to enter a corps which is closed to Jews, half-Jews and friends of Jews, can sign up in our recruitment office at the pay rates determined by the government.' It continues: 'Those volunteers who make themselves known to us do not need to give up their current jobs or professions, because those who are accepted by us will only be inducted into restricted units of suitable troops in order to guarantee Aryan-Germanic purity. However, all volunteers accepted by us must commit themselves in writing and give their oath to be at our disposal at any time and to report for duty as soon as they receive the call.' It continues: 'If someone is prepared to serve at once, they will be provisionally entered into other suitable formations, which are led by officers known to us. He must, however, commit himself to entering our formation as soon as we require it.'

It will be clear to anyone who reads these lines correctly that these volunteer formations and these kinds of part-time volunteers are intended to become the pogrom militia. For this reason, it is illuminating that the Committee for Public Enlightenment pursues its anti-semitic propaganda by all means available among the army and the volunteer corps. The Ministry of War has declared – as one would expect – that it does not support this volunteer formation of the Committee for Public Enlightenment and has prohibited any further recruit-ment. However, recruitment continues in secret and the German People's League in Berlin-Schöneberg is again placing advertisements in which – having become more cautious – it only solicits moral and material support for the Border Defence Force East, to which it has already contributed considerable sums. This is quite open. The more suspicious activities are pursued surreptitiously, since speaking plainly about them is thought to be questionable and tactically unwise.

The military is thus sufficiently organized for pogroms. The question now is to incorporate civilians effectively – as the gentlemen of the Committee for Public Enlightenment thought – and they have acted accordingly. At a secret and very well attended meeting at the Askanische Gymnasium in Berlin, Hallesche Straße, Herr Richard Kunze, for-merly the general secretary of the Conservative Party, now a pioneer of pogrom antisemitism, delivered one of his vile inflammatory speeches against the Jews. In the course of this he produced two rubber truncheons, the 'big Cohn', costing 25 marks, and the 'small Cohn', costing 20,[27] declaring them the best and most beautiful weapons against the Jews. The factory producing them had committed itself to supplying only national-minded men and women (meaning violent antisemites). The jubilant cries of his supporters, the crude death threats against Jews, assured Mr 'Cudgel' Kunze that his meaning had been understood. That was the start.

Then, on 11 July, in front of the Berliner Philharmonie, where the German Nationals held their annual conference, there was a busy distribution of flyers. These suggested that every national-minded person should immediately equip themselves with a rubber truncheon, the effects of which are more terrible than those of the truncheons carried by the British police. Caution is advised so that the truncheons are put only into the right hands (meaning those promoting pogrom antisemitism).

And further: in Herr Kunze's *Deutsche Wochenblatt* there has been an advertisement since 10 July: 'Hey there![28] Anyone who wants to protect themselves against physical assault must get themselves this newly invented and very effective means of defence. Available only to reliable (!!)

persons. Further information from HG 405, office of this newspaper.'

Such things are quietly taking place under the noses of the authorities!

V   *The First Consequences of the Agitation*

Is it any wonder if this shameless rabble-rousing, this constant whipping up of base instincts, this conscious working towards violence, then bears its evil fruit? And wherever things are fermenting, dubious figures appear, making fiery antisemitic speeches and inciting the heated masses to plunder Jewish businesses. That is what happened at the end of June during the unrest in Berlin-N.; that is what happened in Berlin-Schöneberg; that is the news we are hearing from elsewhere. Not only do the newspapers report it, but we know that the relevant authorities are aware of it through their own observations. Who instigated the antisemitic tumult during the second week of July in the seaside resort of Kolberg? The Kolberg city council confirmed at its meeting of 14 July that it was 'not a local', but a penniless student called Banduin, who incited and led it; and that hired combatants were also involved. Anyone not struck blind knows that antisemitic funds were paying these wages. In the Silesian spa of Salzbrunn there were also antisemitic assaults on Jewish visitors. Recently, in the East Prussian seaside resort of Cranz, terrible scenes played out which became so threatening that military assistance had to be requested. This is the extent to which antisemitic agitation has prospered. It seems both silly and suspicious when the Committee for Public Enlightenment suddenly warns its members in one of its leaflets not to let apparently antisemitic agents draw them into the plunder of Jewish businesses. What hypocrisy! Their justification: Jews have paid these agents because they want to stuff their pockets with insurance payouts. As Representative Gröber said recently in the National Assembly: 'No one looks for someone hiding behind a door unless they themselves are doing the same!'

It is telling that the shadows of this uncurbed subversive activity have reached places abroad and received due attention there. The *Neue Zürcher Zeitung*[29] already reported in depth on 15 May about the new antisemitism in Germany. Reliable sources in America inform us that the situation is being followed attentively in political circles – and not only Jewish ones – and that there is concern that republican Germany is out to earn a Polish-style reputation for pogroms for itself. The British occupation authorities in

Cologne are actively promoting the distribution of a public information pamphlet: *Antisemitism in Germany*. Whether these occurrences are helpful for our foreign relations – especially with America – which we should be working hard to maintain; whether this artificially whipped-up antisemitic high tide will harm our foreign relations, must be judged by the Minister for Foreign Affairs.

VI *And Us?*

And now I ask you, you German men and women, what do you say to this shameless agitation, which seeks to put the lives and well-being of thousands of your fellow citizens in extreme danger? Is this the thanks of the fatherland to the thousands upon thousands of Jewish soldiers who shed their life's blood for us all, without considering religion or origins, and who are now beneath cemetery lawns? Is this the consolation offered to the women mourning their spouses, to the children calling for their fathers, to the brides weeping for their betrothed?

We Jews wish that any one of us who harms the German people or our German fatherland be held strictly to account. Which section of the population is made up entirely of saints? But it is a tremendous outrage to agitate irresponsibly for violence against all Jews for the failings of individuals, when the consequences are unforeseeable. Where does that leave morality, where does it leave justice, and how are we to arrive at an orderly reconstruction after the ghastly collapse of the fatherland, if these cornerstones are missing?

But, I keep hearing, surely we must battle against 'Jewish supremacy which has expanded in such an unbridled manner since the revolution'. Now, this talk of 'Jewish supremacy' is a lie designed, by means of constant and loud repetition, to dupe people who cannot think for themselves. It is as much a lie as is the idea that Jews, as capitalists, agitated for the war, then dragged it out, ended it prematurely and were responsible for the enforced peace; that they brought about the revolution; that they are simultaneously capitalists and Bolshevists. A 'Jewish supremacy' only exists in the brains of blinkered antisemitic agitators, and it is a matter of indifference to Judaism as it is to Christianity whether its adherents are active in the government, in shops or in factories.

Both faiths, as indeed the morality of any decent human being, demand that the good be encouraged and the evil resisted. Anyone who does not wish to see the blood of citizens flowing in the streets, or that history should report bestial murders and violence to our descendants must be prepared to fight pogrom antisemitism. Antisemitic rabble-rousing is the precursor of anarchy.

Are we facing pogroms? We are not facing them if right-thinking people reject and fight against them. It is a service to the fatherland to manfully oppose pogrom agitation, which unleashes the worst powers of bad people.

Notes

1   This was the address of the main office of the Central Association of German Citizens of Jewish Faith, which employed Wiener. Today, the site is occupied by the Jewish Museum Berlin.

2   Donald L. Niewyk, the scholar of Jews in Weimar Germany writes: 'The German adjective *völkisch* cannot satisfactorily be translated into a single English word. At once it conveys a sense of nationalism and racial purity combined with a romantic notion of the collective genius of the common people' (*The Jews in Weimar Germany*, Baton Rouge, LA: Louisiana State University Press, 1980, p. 46).

3   Alfred Roth (1879–1948), antisemitic writer and agitator.

4   Friedrich Lange (1852–1917), journalist with the *Deutsche Zeitung* and political activist who sought to build a political platform that combined antisemitism with opposition to Roman Catholicism and Socialism, and promoted a brand of 'pure Germanism' that involved glorification of war, economic self-sufficiency and extreme nationalism.

5   Count Ernst Reventlow (1869–1943), naval officer, writer and extreme right-wing political agitator; Richard Nordhausen (1868–1941), poet, journalist, founder of a rowing club and antisemite; Philipp Stauff (1876–1923), antisemitic author and journalist, who edited the *Semi-Kürschner*, 1911, and was the author of the multi-volume antisemitic encyclopedia *Sigilla veri* (*Seal of Truth*), 1929.

6   Richard Kunze (1872–1945), right-wing politician and antisemitic agitator, known as Knüppel Kunze (Cudgel Kunze). In 1919 he founded an antisemitic newspaper, *Deutsche Wochenblatt*

(*German Weekly*), which he sold from his butcher's shop. In 1920 he joined the German National People's Party, in 1921 he founded the antisemitic German-Social Party and in 1930 he joined the Nazi Party. He served as a member of the Reichstag throughout the Nazi era and disappeared in 1945, presumed dead.

7   Wilhelm Bruhn (1869–1951), publisher and antisemitic agitator. He published the Berlin newspaper *Staatsbürgerzeitung*. In 1900 he used his newspaper to accuse a Jewish butcher of carrying out the ritual murder of an eighteen-year-old boy called Ernst Winter. This led to anti-Jewish violence in the town of Konitz, where the murder took place. Bruhn and his editor were prosecuted for libel and served prison sentences. The exact sense of Wiener's rhetoric here is unclear.

8   The Centre Party represented the Roman Catholic interest and was the second largest party in the early Weimar parliament; the Spartacus League was a revolutionary Marxist group.

9   Georg von Below (1858–1927), economic historian and antisemitic, Pan-German agitator; Houston Stewart Chamberlain (1855–1927), an influential exponent of the theory of 'Aryan' supremacy and antisemitism. His *Foundations of the Nineteenth Century*, published in 1899, greatly influenced far-right thinkers and politicians, including Hitler; Heinrich Claß (1868–1953), president of the Pan-German League and right-wing politician who wrote under the pseudonyms Einhart and Daniel Frymann. His best-known book, *If I Were Kaiser* (1912), advocated the colonization of Eastern Europe and removal of 'inferior' Slavic peoples. He supported Hitler's 1923 Putsch; Prof R. Geyer-Wien – no biographical information is available; Max von Gruber (1853–1927), scientist and eugenics expert, supported the expansion of colonialism and was a member of the Pan-German League; Dietrich Schäfer (1845–1929), academic historian and follower of Heinrich Treitschke and member of the Pan-German League, whom Hitler acknowledged as a precursor; Georg Wilhelm Schiele (1868–1932), surgeon and political activist, member of the Pan-German League, participant in the abortive Kapp Putsch of 1920, close associate of Alfred Hugenberg; Friedrich von Schwerin (1862–1925), Chair of the Regional Council of Frankfurt/Oder; Reinhold Seeberg (1859–1935), Protestant theologian and member of the German National Peoples' Party, author of numerous books.

10 Julius Friedrich Lehmann (1864–1935), influential publisher of medical, *völkisch* and racist books and journals.

11 Walter Liek was a pseudonym of Hans von Liebig (1874–1931), the grandson of the famous chemist Justus von Liebig. Author of numerous far-right and antisemitic works.

12 Georg Davidsohn (1872–1942), author and editor of the Social Democratic journal *Vorwärts* (*Forwards*). Representative in the Reichstag from 1912–18. He died in the Jewish hospital in Berlin in unexplained circumstances.

13 The Border Defence Force East [Grenzschutz Ost] was made up of various volunteer Freikorps groups and militias, initially to protect Germany's border with Poland against incursions arising from the Polish uprising of 1918/9.

14 No biographical information could be found about Werner-Bußbach.

15 This was probably Johannes Joseph Karl (Hans) Knauer (1895–1952), soldier, physician and university lecturer. Active in various far-right groups during the Weimar Republic. Joined the Nazi Party in 1931 and the SA in 1933.

16 This was the address of the Committee for Public Enlightenment.

17 Artur Dinter (1876–1948), writer and far-right politician. He published a three-volume antisemitic novel, rooted in his Roman Catholic faith, *The Sins of the Time* [*Die Sünden der Zeit*]. Joined the Nazi Party very early – his party membership was number 5 – but later broke with the Nazis, who mistrusted him after they came to power and even arrested him.

18 The original refers to 'Radauantisemitismus' (violent antisemitism), a topic of widespread public debate in Weimar Germany, as antisemitism rapidly became more radical and extreme.

19 During the war, a debate began about political representation of consumers in society, which raged in the early years of the Weimar Republic. For antisemites, international capitalism, department stores and consumer associations were evidence of 'Jewish' efforts to undermine the nation and *völkisch* values. The meaning of the last sentence is obscure, but may be suggesting the Federation regrets being unable to drive prices up to a level its members would benefit from.

20 The original phrase 'zum Zweck der Ziegenwurstfabrikation' is taken to mean that it is nonsensical and without basis in reality.

21 An editorial note inserted into the text at this point reads, 'In the *Umschau*, the previous edition of this magazine'.

22 *Rundkopf* – derogatory term of unknown origin, possibly a reference to circumcision.

23 Heinrich Pudor (1865–1943), writer, vegetarian, naturist, travel writer and antisemitic agitator who sold his father's musical conservatory to establish an antisemitic publishing house. After the election of 1912 he focused on antisemitic agitation and founded a newspaper, *Antisemitisches Rüstzeug des Deutschen Volksrats* (*Antisemitic Armour of the German People's Council*), which was succeeded in 1918 by *Treu Deutsch: Nachrichten des Deutschen Volksrats* (*True German: News of the German People's Council*), presumably the paper Wiener refers to. The German People's Council is thought to have been a figment of Pudor's imagination.

24 The original, *Mistgabel*, is more derogatory as it carries the suggestion that the pitchfork is reserved for work on dung heaps.

25 The flyer is entitled *No. 15: Wake-Up Call for German Fellow Citizens* [*Weckruf Deutsche Volksgenossen*]. At the foot of the flyer is printed: 'Sent to numerous government offices and all newspapers'.

26 Lehnin Abbey was a Cistercian monastery founded in 1180 and dissolved in the sixteenth century. The prophecy comprises 100 rhyming couplets and appeared in the seventeenth century purporting to be the work of Hermann von Lehnin, a fourteenth-century monk.

27 Kunze named his own weapon 'Heda' (See Donald Niewyk, *Socialist, Antisemite and Jew* (Baton Rouge, LA: Louisiana State University Press, 1971, p. 71). I am grateful to my colleague Sigrid Klinge for deciphering this.

28 The original is 'Heda!', which makes a pun on the name Kunze gave to his own weapon.

29 A Swiss German-language newspaper, founded in 1780.

German Jewry in Political, Economic and Cultural Perspective

LECTURE

Deputy Syndic of the Central Association
of German Citizens of Jewish Faith

Dr Alfred Wiener

IN DESSAU ON 25 JANUARY 1924

Philo Verlag, Berlin SW 68, Lindenstraße 13

Motto: If someone disputes my claim on my German fatherland, he disputes my right to my thoughts, my feelings, to the language that I speak and the air that I breathe. That is why I must defend myself against him – as against a murderer.

Gabriel Rießer[1]

LADIES AND GENTLEMEN! I have the honour to speak to you in the name of the Central Association of German Citizens of Jewish Faith [Centralverein deutscher Staatsbürger jüdischen Glaubens].[2] The Central Association is Germany's largest union of German Jews; it has 65,000 members and represents around 300,000 Jews who are members of Jewish communities and associations.

It is not unimportant for our conversation to establish at once that there are 600,000 Jews scattered among a population of 65 million Germans.

The Central Association stands as a defence against all unjustified attacks on German Jewry, attacks on Jewish teachings and anything that is unjustifiably levelled against Jews. Self-examination requires that we continue our effort to educate our members to be full Germans (where that is not already the case). For this reason, the first paragraph of our Constitution states that it is our mission to strengthen our members 'in the unwavering cultivation of a German cast of mind'. That means that the Central Association of German Citizens of Jewish Faith takes a healthy German-patriotic position. It is, I wish to add, completely neutral in relation to politics and religion.

The purpose of today's meeting is to discuss the Jewish question calmly and dispassionately with the leadership of Dessau, from all political camps. It seems to us necessary that this leading class should have the opportunity to form an impression of how a German Jew, one for whom the word 'fatherland' is not a hollow concept, expresses himself about the Jewish question and about the allegations levelled against German Jewry.

Under these circumstances we felt it right not to hold an open public meeting. Our view is – and I hope and believe that those present from all camps will agree – that the current atmosphere is not conducive to having a calm and objective discussion of the Jewish question in a public meeting to which anyone could gain entrance with the intention of being disruptive.

We consider it to be quite wrong to enter into argument with those opponents of the Jews who are generally described as violent antisemites.[3] Truly, I have no doubt whatever that many among those who are '*völkisch*' – who, for the most part, love their fatherland just as much as those from other factions, and who are honest with themselves and serious about the fatherland – reject such violent antisemitism. But you will agree with me: the danger of a public meeting is that these violent antisemites will take over and seize the opportunity to disturb the calm and objectivity of the discussion.

As for my method, I will strive to remain strictly objective. The quotations I will cite are taken wherever possible from the Christian side and from right-wing factions. I will not use any quotations that relate to some chance event or some irrelevant person – as was apparently the case in a recent newspaper article by an esteemed clerical figure from Dessau. And I am able to say for myself that I have engaged seriously with the problems we are talking about here, out of a deep love for Germany and for Judaism, and not merely for the sake of this meeting or my office.

If we examine the accusations that are made today against German Jews, it is advisable to adopt a method that, according to Johannes Scherr, has sadly been lost among the Germans, namely the study of history.[4]

We must climb down into history. And if we do this, then we see that in the course of world history, and particularly in three specific epochs, the selfsame accusations were levelled against certain groups of people that are today levelled against the Jews.

One of the most interesting periods in world history is the epoch when Christianity first emerged, a time which the great Adolf von Harnack rendered so vividly in his various masterful works, a time presented to the German-speaking world in an equally masterful way by the theologian Schürer in his *History of the People of Israel in the Time of Jesus Christ*.[5]

The accusations made against the new Christianity at that time were very like the accusations of our day made against the Jews. If you study the works of the Church Fathers – sadly they are given far too little attention – you will see in Augustine, in Athenagoras but above all in the *Apologeticum* of Tertullian that exactly the same accusations that are levelled against German Jews today – against Jews generally – were made by the Romans, by the declining heathen world, against the Christians. For example, the new Christians were rigorously denied Roman citizenship with the accusation that they were not Roman at all, that they were foreigners who were spreading mischief in the Roman Empire. Tertullian writes complainingly: 'Treacherous assassins surround the Emperor Nero, but they count as good Romans – however, we who strive to render unto Caesar what is Caesar's, we are regarded as strangers, as of foreign birth, as an alien race who do not belong to the great Roman fatherland.' Now, Ladies and Gentlemen, you can see, even from this one accusation, how history repeats itself.

Then we can examine a second large group in world history which has had to bear – like the Jews – similar, in fact identical, accusations. These are the Catholics, especially during the time of the so-called Culture War [*Kulturkampf*].[6] Anyone wishing to engage seriously with these matters should study the outstanding history of the Culture War by Kießling [*sic*].[7] Whoever does will be forced to the conclusion that at that time, in the 1870s, the Catholics were subjected to exactly the same allegations as the Jews today.

Let me read to you one example out of dozens of documents that support my claim.

If you open the *Allgemeine Zeitung* of 5 December 1870 you will find an essay, 'A Wish for the Kaiser's Coronation':

'Everything would be blessed, if a poisonous fungus were not eating at our entrails, carrying out its destructive work ceaselessly, day and night. It is unnecessary to say what the sickness is: the elections to the Prussian Regional Parliament have again exposed the wound; whoever does not shrink back in horror must be blind. The most flourishing, enlightened, lively part of Germany – Rhineland and Westphalia – has sent 40 ultramontane representatives to the regional government.[8] Truly, a major battle lost on the Loire would be a smaller misfortune for our nation than this defeat… Thus the silent conspiracy against state and civilization grows and grows, hour by hour, sending its grasping tendrils over everything to suffocate us in due course.'

The following is, in my view, a still more dramatic proof of what I wish to demonstrate. The time of the World War is unfortunately slipping further and further from the memory of the present day. It is extremely important and valuable for us Germans to recall the accusations that our former enemies levelled against us during the war. There are very interesting and highly regarded books about this; I will mention only the oeuvre of the outstanding Berlin university professor Dr Troeltsch, who died recently.[9] Troeltsch identifies two kinds of invective against the German people used in the literature of our enemies, in the newspapers and writings of our former opponents. He terms them 'literature of the first degree' and of the 'second degree'. In the literature of the first degree it is claimed that the Germans are anthropologically inferior and culturally base; in other words, precisely the same things that are said today of the Jews, especially according to the theory of Chamberlain![10] Just as Chamberlain claimed that all important figures in world history have been Germanic, and had brought culture from India to Spain and from the deserts of Africa all the way to the northern lands, so the enemies of Germany claim that it was not the Germans who made great inventions and perfected supreme cultural achievements, but their own people, i.e. those of the hostile states. For this reason, because the Germans are anthropologically and culturally inferior – according to the derogatory claims of our enemies – they must be robbers and child murderers, they must have raped women in Belgium, they must be Boches. 'Boches', this strange word, designed to express contempt for Germans as an inferior race.

You will concede the word 'Jew' echoes all this; that the same accusations are made against the German Jews. Yes, it is demonstrable that every slogan that is hostile to Jews can be turned into one hostile to Germans. Thus, the 'striving for world domination' which today is said of the Jews was, during the war, chalked up to the Germans almost daily in the enemy press; and thus the Belgian professor Delaville tried to establish, in a work of art history, that the

Germans are an entirely inferior race, incapable of creating any sublime works of lasting value. And that leads to the further conclusion: since the Germans are not capable of accomplishing anything truly creative, all they can do is to imitate, in an inferior way, the intellectual achievements of those who came before them (something the Jews are accused of daily by the *völkisch* faction)…!

Further examples on this topic: I imagine you will know of the founder of modern philology, one of the most important philologists of all, August Wolff [*sic*], who died in 1824.[11] He was accused by a highly regarded French philologist called Bérard of copying his groundbreaking study of Homer from French authors, specifically d'Aubignac.[12] Röntgen had, according to similar writings, probably stolen his discovery from French colleagues.[13] This might not have been proven by any actual evidence; but it was clear that everything achieved in X-ray research in Germany during the war had been mere plagiarism. If the names Wolff [*sic*] or Röntgen were erased and the name Einstein, who is known to be a Jew, inserted, you would see that exactly the same claims are made in books, pamphlets and leaflets that are hostile to the Jews.

You may still recall from the war that our former enemies disputed our claim to a number of great men.

During the war, Czech newspapers and booklets but also academic books laid claim to Lessing, Schiller, Goethe and Nietzsche, and also Caprivi,[14] whose name was actually Coprivor, according to Czech sources. They also claimed – naturally – Count Zeppelin, who originated from the house of Cepeline, and who Germanized himself and contributed to the fame of the German people.

You will find the selfsame thoughts among our *völkisch* opponents.

It is very funny – to demonstrate where such things lead – that the English press claimed that the highly decorated Field Marshal von Mackensen wasn't German at all and was in the last analysis of British descent: 'MacKensen'.[15] And because coincidence can be whimsical, I'd like to point out that, according to the *Semi-Gotha* – a register published by the *völkisch* side, listing members of the German nobility and aristocracy who are related to Jews, or are alleged to have Jewish blood in their veins – Mackensen is supposed to be of Jewish origin. There is a note at the end of the *Semi-Gotha*: 'PS: The article about the family of the Prussian Cavalry General, August von Mackensen, was inadvertently not printed, and is also missing from previous sections on the military nobility.'

How far the *völkisch* side go to – if I may express it

thus – put the blood-history of leading figures among the German people under the microscope has been shown very clearly and to general astonishment in a book which I would like to present to you briefly. It is the so-called *Semi-Imperator*,[16] published by those who have produced others of these '*Semi*' books, the *Semi-Alliancen*[17] and the *Semi-Gotha*.[18] This *Semi-Imperator* proves on the basis of apparently scholarly material, such as genealogies and various photographs, that the unhappy Kaiser Wilhelm II has Jewish blood in his veins and that this is the reason for the misfortune that has descended on the fatherland. This Jewish blood allegedly entered the house of the Hohenzollern through the late Queen of Great Britain and Ireland, Victoria, who had illicit congress with a Jewish physician, Wolf.[19] I am not saying this to make a bad joke: you will find this insult alongside the genealogy and photographs presented in this book with all due scholarly seriousness.

As a further proof of just how similar the views of our enemies concerning the German people are to the views of the opponents of the Jews, consider this:

Chamberlain states in his witty, but in my view frightful, *Foundations of the Nineteenth Century* that an uneducated child could recognize a Jew by smell alone.

And now: in the Parisian *Medical News* (*Gazette médicale de Paris* no. 267 of 24 June 1915), a French physician, Dr Bérillon, makes the assertion that German soldiers, especially the injured, can be recognized immediately by smell as German.[20] I need hardly add that we can only smile contemptuously at such 'science'. But one thing is certain: that precisely the same supposed findings are applied to the Germans as our *völkisch* opponents apply to the Jews.

We can, cautiously, draw one conclusion from these three parallel examples: these accusations are of a kind levelled against minorities again and again throughout history. They arose against the early Christians who were in the minority in the Roman world, against the Catholic minority from Protestant circles and equally against the Germans during the World War.

I wanted to say this by way of introduction, before embarking on my main topic.

You will understand if, in view of stories in the Dessau press concerning the Jews, I must refer to the basic idea which always comes up, namely the so-called 'Jewish spirit'.

This Jewish spirit is, according to the *völkisch*, not native, not rooted in the soil. There is something unhealthy, corrosive, something corruptly international about it;

something that tears things down, that always inclines radically to the political left; something decidedly materialistic; something (the word has been used) anti-Germanic. One could say: the Jewish spirit is understood in *völkisch* circles to be the opposite of what Richard Wagner termed the German spirit: 'Being German means doing a thing for its own sake.' Therefore, in light of this *völkisch* conception, 'being Jewish means only doing something for a specific material gain'.

Therefore, we must deal with the key issue: the concepts 'national' and 'international' in the language of the *völkisch*: Aryan-idealistic and Jewish-materialistic, or right-wing national, left-wing international. When dealing with this question, we should first ask ourselves, 'Why, in fact, are Jews to be found by preference in left-leaning parties, which are allegedly not trustworthy from the nationalist point of view?'

In fact, it is not even correct that there are no Jews in parties of the right, although there are not large numbers. Yet it is a truism that the creator of the German conservative world view was the Jew Friedrich Stahl, who was called Schlesinger before his baptism.[21] It almost strikes one as comic when Bluntschli[22] writes in his *History of Constitutional Law*:

'It is basically the Semitic world view which is revived once more in Stahl's philosophy of the state and the law... It is perhaps the most fully developed application of that particular fundamental religious view of state and law.'

Perhaps I may remind you that men such as Lasker and Bamberger played a leading role in the precursor of the German People's Party [Deutsche Volkspartei], the National Liberal Party [Nationalliberale Partei].[23] If membership was not denied to Jews by the party manifesto, we would surely find them in the German National People's Party [Deutschnationale Volkspartei]. After all, it would be peculiar if a people of such decided conservatism as the Jews, who have guarded their religion and traditions through millennia, should suddenly be no longer inclined to support parties which claim to uphold the conservative tradition. It is dishonest if we blame Jews today for not being represented in the right-wing parties to the extent that they are in the left, because they have never been wanted in the right-wing parties.

In 1910 the main organ of the Conservative Party, the *Kreuz-Zeitung*, published an article about the so-called Tivoli Manifesto of the Conservatives and included this extraordinarily interesting point:

'The large majority of the Conservative Party has become persuaded that the antisemitic passage of its manifesto cannot practically be justified any longer. After all, there are conservative forces alive and active in Jewry, as we see from the heartening example of countless Jewish men in daily life, in the sciences and the arts, while those destructive forces so noticeable among Jews have unfortunately also developed to a great extent among racially pure Germans.'[24]

This quotation, from an authoritative source, is particularly compelling for those who do not view things entirely through the lens of party politics. It shows quite clearly that, before the 'inflation of hate', the national sympathies of the German Jews were judged differently from today. It is – let us think of the loss of Posen[25] – a wistful but helpful reminder that in the Reichstag election of a man such as the current German National [Peoples' Party] leader Count Westarp, it was Jews who played a decisive role.[26] For his election (a 600-vote majority) in the district of Bomst-Meseritz was only possible because the Jews living in the east decidedly supported the Conservative candidate because he was the candidate of Germandom [*Deutschtum*] against the Poles – despite their serious reservations about the Tivoli Manifesto.

Few words have fallen prey to such misuse as 'fatherland' and 'national'. For every German of every party who declares himself for the fatherland in any way at all, these words ought to be the holiest and dearest, something he feels and lives by, but about which he does not speak.

Is it conducive to the development of the Reich and its constituent states that the sacred word 'national', in particular, has acquired a distinctly party-political character, so that it appears divisive rather than unifying?

In fact, this word 'national' did not by any means always have the meaning which parties attribute to it today, as though it were self-evident. You will find that, at the time of the Stein-Hardenberg reform, those circles opposed to reform were precisely those which now so ardently stress the importance of the national, namely the large landowners.[27] And yet, viewed from the present time, this reform was an entirely national and patriotic act. But in 1808 this reform was characterized by, among others, the landowner Freiherr von der Marwitz, the 'leader of the rebels', as he was described in one essay, as the 'revolutionizing of the fatherland', as the 'war of crass materialism against the divine order.'[28] I particularly ask you to take note of this accusation of 'crass materialism' which is being laid at the door of the Jews today in such a derogatory manner. In this context it is interesting to examine a petition submitted by members of the nobility of the Brandenburg districts of Lebus, Storkow and Beeskow against the Hardenberg reform. The indignation of the nobility regarding the introduction of the reform is expressed in strong terms in this document and it states literally – you will be astonished! – 'One wishes to make a modern Jewish State out of our old, noble Prussia!' This was already being said in 1807, when the alleged 'decisive Jewish question' did not even exist in Prussia–Germany... And then think of the forceful opposition, which came from certain conservatives, from certain high military figures, from certain large landowners, to the formation of the Reich by the old Kaiser and Bismarck. Read the memoir and correspondence of Herr von Rauch, the equerry of King Wilhelm, a man who had influence at the General Headquarters.[29] Even von Roon was a decided opponent of the coronation of the Kaiser and described these events disparagingly as 'unnecessary and something that is likely to harm the Prussian state'.[30]

You might say – with some justification – that I am ignoring the fact that among the parties of the left the

Jewish element is particularly strong. And because radical parties are usually found in opposition, and are critical of all that currently exists and strive to change things, one blames the Jews in these parties for this stance. On the other hand, it is said that Jews are attracted by this subversive tendency through some spiritual affinity. This has been claimed in relation to Bolshevism more than any other radical political movement, and we will use this often cited example to examine the apparent but also the actual relationship between Bolshevism and Jewry.

Tsarist Russia was hell for the Russian Jew. In recent Russian history there were steps made towards political progress, economic development, cultural advancement. Only for the Jew, time appeared to stand still. For him, the Middle Ages continued, with all their horrors. I ask that you take this quite literally. I do not have to go back to the last century and describe the times of Alexander I, who was described by Alexander Herzen as 'Genghis Khan with the telegraph'.[31] Events have taken place in Russia in our century which are painful to relate. I would like to read to you from a scholarly book by Professor Léo Errera, a Catholic from Brussels, which paints a scene from one of the typical anti-Jewish pogroms:

'The unfortunate ones had their tongues torn out using

pliers, their eyes put out, their hands, feet, noses and ears cut off – these events were witnessed by Dr Dorozevski, physician in the city hospital, a Christian. An elderly Jewish man had his belly cut open and stuffed with bed feathers after his intestines had been removed. Women and children were hurled from second-floor windows into the streets amid the raucous laughter of the crowds. Young women and even children were violated, some died on the spot and others went mad.'[32]

Is it any wonder, then, if Russian Jews did *not* use all their energies to promote the furtherance of these circumstances; that they were *not* followers of those political groups which protected the existing system and powers that kept them in oppression and darkness? Consider also those female Jewish students who could only remain at certain Russian universities if they registered themselves as prostitutes. Yet nothing could be more erroneous than the presumption that the ranks of the Russian revolution were entirely made up of the Jewish intelligentsia. In 1900, in the *Prussian Yearbooks*, published by the right-leaning Professor Delbrück, Emil Daniels reviewed the biography of the famous Count Kropotkin, the father of nihilism.[33] The book teems with the names of young members of high and highest aristocracy, who were as sick of the demands of their rank as they were of being under the tutelage of the government, and who banded together to forge a new Russia. I don't want to go too far into these questions, although it would be tempting to demonstrate just how the philosophy of Hegel became seminal for the spiritual make-up of the revolutionary Russians; as were Büchner, Moleschott, Vogt and not least Wilhelm Marr – who has the honour of being both the father of modern German antisemitism and of Bolshevism.[34]

I just want to go into one more matter. When the Bolshevik revolution was victorious and it was widely feared that it would spread to the remaining states, certain circles claimed – in order to deflect public opinion – that the Bolshevik government was overwhelmingly made up of Jews or perhaps those who had been Jews, so that a victory for Bolshevism was tantamount to a victory for the Jewish world government. Is that true?

In 1921 the antisemitic press published an account of the make-up of the Russian government. It stated that 703 men made up the Russian government, of whom 664 were Jews. The remainder were Russians, Latvians, Germans, Armenians, Poles, Czechs, etc. These claims were supported with a lot of detail, so that they created the impression of being true. However, those familiar with the actual circumstances in Russia did not know what to make of these numbers. For there are only eighteen People's Commissars, and they alone could claim to make up the government. Of these, it was estimated about two years ago, only two were Jews – Lev Bronstein-Trotsky and Dovgalevsky[35] – one administering the War Commissariat and Navy, the other the Commissariat for Post and Telegraphy. So they went further and also counted the Jewish officials in the eighteen People's Commissariats who made up the second rank. But here only seven Jews were found, while the total number of officials ranged from 126 to 162. Finally, every single name given in the anti-Jewish press was analysed. And there they found the solution to the puzzle. The authors had randomly chosen 703 names from the vast number of Russian officials; the initial selection was of 664 Jews, and then – to mask the forgery somewhat – they added a few non-Jews. If we take note of all of those who have a job as an official in Russia – and in a purely Socialist state that is very many – then the number of 664 Jews is actually surprisingly small.

It is not my intention to say a single word in favour of Communism or Bolshevism. I only wish to remind you that as early as 1920 a pamphlet was published: *Protest of the German Jews against Communism*, by Professor Herzog, in which leading German Jews expressed their opposition to the Communist and Bolshevist world view.[36] But it seemed to me to be necessary to illuminate these complex questions for the sake of clarity.

Allow me now to make some remarks about quotations and quoting. This is necessary because an esteemed theological authority of Dessau is known to have taken his proofs mostly from quotations. How is it possible to believe that the dance around the golden calf had something to do with greed for gold or with materialism? For it is not about the dance around the *golden* calf but about the golden *calf*! When Moses was away from the people and his brother was in charge of priestly business, the people fell back into the Egyptian worship of false idols. They joyfully offered their treasures and precious objects in order to create this idol and to pray to it – not because it was gold but because it was a calf, an animal deity with which the people were familiar from their time in Egypt. It was the opposite of the common *völkisch* conception of the dance of the Jews around the golden calf.

It seems to me, even after just this examination, that one can 'prove' far more with quotations than one can, say, with statistics, which are after all also a popular way of 'proving' certain things. I want to make the claim that I can put together a series of quotations from the works of that great master Goethe, which will expose his real character as the greatest hater of Germans ever to have lived. One can do the same experiment with Frederick the Great. Recently a French pamphlet circulated in the Rhine region, published under the title *La France et le pays rhénan* [*France and the Rhine Country*].[37] It bears as an epigraph a passage that can be found in the memoirs of Frederick the Great, written in French naturally, which reads:

'On its eastern side France only has those borders which it can claim by virtue of its moderation and its justice. It would be desirable if the Rhine could continue to form the border of this monarchy.'

Now, just imagine all the things one could 'prove' with this quotation! But such stolen proofs are only allowed against us. One takes a random quotation from a still-living Jew which disparages German Jewry, 'proving' that 'the Jews' have this or that attitude! Or one takes some quotation or other from the past, out of context, and this is supposed to show how the Jews of today think! We ask for quotations only from Jews who play a leading role in Jewry today! We will not tolerate it if quotations from some writer or editor who has not the slightest connection with Jews are pinned on us. What would we say if an Englishman or a Frenchman or an American were to take the minutes of the Reichstag, extracting from them speeches by Communist or *völkisch* representatives and making the claim: 'This is the spirit of the German people!'

With this method we can prove everything and nothing.

I would like to offer just a few quotations. You will be surprised, for example, to read Treitschke – highly regarded today by the German-*völkisch* faction, and in any case a figure deserving regard, whatever you may think of him – writing the following about Bismarck in 1863:

'When I hear a witless *Junker* like this Bismarck bragging about iron and blood because he wants to subjugate Germany, it seems to me that his meanness of spirit is only exceeded by his absurdity.'[38]

Who would entertain the idea – unless he has evil intent – of taking this view as representing that of the German or monarchical spirit? But similar things are said against us daily, especially in the essay of that clerical – though not malicious – personality from Dessau. Here is a statement from Eugen Dühring, the well-known philosopher, on whom our German-*völkisch* opponents often draw. He once wrote, in the *Moderner Völkergeist*, 1899, No. 11:

'Recently, someone in the German Reichstag tried to wangle 50,000 marks in order to erect a memorial to

Herr von Goethe in Strasbourg in honour of all things German. Social Democrats, the impertinent and in general the liberals know why they want to lead the people astray with this servile, pornography-loving Frankfurt sprout and Weimar court poet.'[39]

This was said by a well-known German *völkisch* authority. But we would be obstinate, we would be following a false and reprehensible methodology – one that has been and is used daily against us Jews – if we then claimed that this was indeed the view of Goethe taken by serious people from the German-*völkisch* side!

Now I would like to make the counter-argument and then we will see whether, after sharing with you some impeccable and trustworthy materials, you think that what I tell you about the national spirit of the German Jews or about the 'Jewish spirit' is anti-national or 'subversive'.

After the war a book appeared from the pen of the well-known German *völkisch* leader Alfred Roth, *The Participation of the Jews in the World War.*[40] In it the claim is made that up to November 1916 only about 4,000 Jews died in action. This assertion rested on statistics procured at that time by the Minister of War von Stein.[41]

Now, if only 4,000 Jews fell – and actually there are certain *völkisch* meetings at which it is claimed that not a single

Jew had even been at the front – then naturally it would mean that the German Jews had not fulfilled their duty to their fatherland, which they were absolutely bound to do.

But this is not at all how it was.

The German Jews, and particularly the Central Association of German Citizens of Jewish Faith, took on the task of compiling an indisputable statistical war record. Every Jewish soldier and fallen soldier had a personnel card, which can be inspected in Berlin. From these irreproachable statistics we see that German Jewry did not lose 4,000 but 12,000 soldiers.

It may actually be said that even the figure of 12,000 is not sufficient for the German Jews; it ought to have been at least 13,500 if set against the total number of Germans who fell. That is right. In fact, the number of fallen German Jews remains around 1,500 lower than the expected percentage of Jews among the total number of fallen. Why is that?

There exists a little-known, strictly scientific work, *Confessional War Statistics*, by R. May.[42] In it the author reveals that, even under the Empire, more Catholics were fit for active service than Protestants, and consequently the number of Catholic war dead is greater than the number of Protestants. That is undoubtedly correct!

For circumstances are in fact such that the population of the rural districts produces, in percentage terms, the highest number of those fit for active service, because they are physically stronger. But in Germany this population is predominantly Catholic, while the Protestant population is concentrated in the cities, specifically the large cities, and works mainly in industry. You will all know that the physical fitness of industrial workers is considerably lower when compared with agricultural workers. So when we return to the topic we are discussing, one could make the slightly odd but accurate claim that the number of Protestants among the German war dead is lower than that of the Catholics! However, it would be a claim from which no one would draw a value judgement. But when it comes to the Jews, they do. Among the Jews the number of those unfit for active service is higher than among the Protestants and Catholics. The Jews, by virtue of their work, are predominantly city dwellers and because of their jobs as businessmen are not as suited for military service as their Christian fellow citizens.

Recently a leading German *völkisch* representative, the Munich-based author Dietrich Eckart, died.[43] He once organized a competition: anyone who could name a Jewish mother who had three sons on the front line for three weeks would receive a prize of 1,000 marks, a considerable sum at that time. When Rabbi Dr Freund from Hanover submitted a list of twenty such families, Eckart declined to pay the promised sum.[44] He was made to pay, because a court judged the claim proved; at the hearing Dr Freund demonstrated not only that twenty Jewish families had three sons on the front line for three weeks, he provided a list of fifty Jewish families who had up to eight sons on the front line of battle for three weeks.

This proof is telling. And if one then says: Yes, the Jews were forced to take part in the war, still they have done nothing that could in any way be described as brave, then I must point out that when it comes to bravery, the Jews held their own. I refer you just to one book: *Jewish Pilots in the War*, by Dr Felix Theilhaber,[45] in which you will read 'that the well-known fighter pilot Frankl, of Jewish origin, was decorated with the Pour le Mérite. The pilot Rosin was also a Jew and Rosin managed to bomb an enemy emplacement after his plane was struck, and met his death when his plane crashed into the fire he had started with his bombs.'

At least twelve Jews also served under Lettow-Vorbeck in the colonial war, four of whom fell.[46] It goes without saying that Jews are taking part in the resistance battle on the Rhine and Ruhr and have also been sent to prison and tortured, admittedly in smaller numbers than other Germans because, as is generally known, Jews are not usually officials.[47] In Upper Silesia and Poland Jews have suffered exactly as much as the rest of the German population, their Christian countrymen. Judicial Councillor Placzek, leader of the city council in Posen, and our council member in Posen, Judicial Councillor Kirschner, have had to experience every form of martyrdom in Polish camps for many weeks.[48]

In Rybnik, the sixth-former Haase, the son of our Representative there, was shot by Polish murderers for being a German messenger.

Jews were not only represented in the Soviet government of Munich; they were in the opposition too. Two Jewish students who belonged to the 'white' troops for the liberation of Munich were severely wounded and died.

Among the Munich hostages who were murdered so inhumanely was the Jewish painter Professor Ernst Berger.[49]

And finally I would like to remind you – as evidence for my claim that German Jewry is to be found in all camps – that Count Arco, who assassinated Eisner, is Jewish on his mother's side; for his mother was born von Oppenheim in Cologne![50]

These facts are concealed when the case is against the Jews. For they do not support the claim that Jews are only to be found in international movements. They certainly wouldn't support the claim that everything that is done or not done by all Jews is anti-German.

The fact that German Jews voluntarily chose death when they experienced the terrible collapse of the German fatherland is attested by the suicide of the well-known jurist Adolf Weißler of Halle, founder of the Union of German Notaries, who, according to his suicide note, shot himself because:

'I cannot bear to live any longer. Believe me that no other reason has driven me than the grief I feel for the deep shame of our people, nothing else. It is better to die than to live. You children may still experience better days, us old ones not. I can't do otherwise. God help me!'[51]

His last request was that his gravestone should be inscribed with the words: 'He did not want to survive the shame of his people.'

A young student, Maximilian Spaeth of Munich, also reached for his revolver after his old friends refused further contact with him because he was a member of the Jewish race (as it is always referred to), leaving him, as he felt, stripped of honour and reputation. He shot himself and wrote in his last testament:

'So only one thing remains to me: that through my death it can be acknowledged that a German of Jewish birth, who believed himself to have striven all his life after the high ideals of humanity and nationhood, despite all his vices and faults, can also be a man of decency and honour. It is my burning wish, which I take to my grave, that Germany and its poor, blind people will one day be free from all the bindings that now rob it of sight, and may rise again to strength and flowering, better than in the past and more immortal in duration and achievement.'

Such statements are suppressed, and are not mentioned in newspaper reports.

Now I will not go so far as our opponents with their twisted methodology, and claim that all Jews are ultra-patriotic. I only claim that neither are all Christians. The decisive issue is that we as German Jews are not better or worse than the world around us.

Now a few words about a question which echoes through all the *völkisch* accusations against German Jewry: international banking and stock market capitalism.

You will know that there is a viewpoint derived from the literature about the *Elders of Zion*: in Germany after the war Jews found a way to achieve supremacy.[52] Jews are established everywhere; this cannot be a coincidence, there must be a purpose and plan behind it: behind all of this stands Jewish world domination – and international Jewish capitalism has set itself the goal of creating world domination by shattering the *völkisch* destiny of other people.

I must start by answering this question: is it true that such a Jewish world government exists, a group of international Jewish capitalists, united for better or for worse? It is a commonplace that is believed in as firmly as the daily rising of the sun. I want to try to let the facts speak for themselves.

A book is lying before me, which has only recently seen the light of day: *Corporations of the Metal Industry* (Stuttgart, 1923).[53] In this book, for the first time, you can find out how all the gigantic businesses in Germany, and particularly in heavy industry, were formed. You can learn in what small measure Jewish capital is involved in these mammoth companies, which today make up the bulk of, and indeed dominate, the German economy. It is not at all my intention to say anything against heavy industry; this is something that is of no concern to the Central Association of German Citizens of Jewish Faith. If you leaf through this book of companies, you will find the Stinnes Corporation. I have always imagined this to be very large. But what you will discover about its undertakings, investments and subsidiaries exceeds all expectations. The Stinnes Corporation has the closest possible relations with the Siemens-Rhein-Elbe-Schuckert-Union. And these large companies, these gigantic companies have feelers everywhere in Germany, everywhere in the world; not only in mining, but in the coal industry; not only in plastics, but in the paper industry, and today to a considerable degree in the newspaper industry, in banking and stock exchanges, in shipping and so on. When I say this at German-*völkisch* meetings, the reply is: 'We are fighting capitalism wherever we find it. But the decisive matter lies elsewhere. The decisive matter is that the Jew controls the banking industry, that he goes to the stock exchange, earns money effortlessly, stuffs his pockets with it and lives high on the hog. The Christian industrialist Stinnes, on the other hand, only makes money in order to keep the German worker employed, to raise the esteem of German trade and industry.' Whoever says this is boundlessly naive. Because the huge development of these corporations – whether you fight them or support them – has only been possible because they have understood how to intertwine their interests with those of the banks. If, for example,

you read in this book that the Stinnes Corporation is in
the closest contact with the Barmer Bankverein, with the
Berliner Handels-Gesellschaft [Berlin Trading Company],
with the Deutsche Kreditsicherungs AG [German Credit
Protection Corporation] and suchlike, you can see from
these bare facts (I will not even refer to share purchases)
how these corporations are bound up with the banks. And
it is also interesting to look into the boards of these giant
undertakings!

One of the most respected German mining companies
is the Gelsenkirchener. The board of this company is made
up of thirty people, among them are two or three Jews,
perhaps even four or five – but also Dr Alfred Hugenberg,
one of the best-known German nationalist representatives,
and Herr Kirdorf, who makes no secret of his antisemitic
persuasion.[54]

If you leaf further through the book you will also find
some Jewish businesses, modest when measured against the
Christian heavy industrial companies – such as, for example, Aquila–Adler, Tellus. Beside the Christian Klöckner
Corporation is the Otto-Wolff Corporation (the head is
a Christian, the second in command is a Jew), the Stumm
Corporation, and so forth. It is not the case that international capital and international industry is in Jewish hands.

These corporations have understood perfectly the value of establishing themselves in other countries. Wherever you look in the world, in Russia, Spain, Finland, etc., Stinnes, Klöckner, Stumm and other German corporations have their investments, their branches, their subsidiary groups. You will find these large, esteemed firms everywhere. And I confess that I enjoy seeing German company names when I'm abroad.

Albert Ballin, a man who flew the German flag honourably throughout the whole world and whose superb German ships beat the English competition, is forgotten today.[55] Jews such as him are also 'internationalist', and Albert Ballin is perhaps among the 300 men seen by our opponents as – in Rathenau's completely misinterpreted expression – ruling the world.[56]

Allow me briefly to say a word about what is seen as the essential 'Jewish spirit', which is alleged in some sections of the German press to be rampant on the German stage in all sorts of smutty plays and unappetizing jokes and in a subversive critical style which runs strongly counter to Germanic nature.

It is curious that, in this connection, when one is speaking of the Jewish spirit, a certain right-wing newspaper is not included.

Why is it not mentioned that one of the largest right-wing German newspapers, read today by thousands of families, is run by Jews? Why? Because this newspaper has a party-political stance which is agreeable to certain German-*völkisch* circles. Many right-wing newspapers – including the *Deutsche Zeitung* – use a well-known right-wing press agency in Berlin whose publisher is of Jewish origin, but who clearly has no 'Jewish spirit'. We must be clear: whatever does not chime with certain party-political inclinations, especially *völkisch* inclinations, is held up as being 'Jewified'. And this is not new.

Friedrich Wilhelm IV, who was the declared enemy of all revolutions, saw a danger in *William Tell*. He said: '*William Tell* is a play for Jews and revolutionaries!'

This term, 'Jewified', is much loved today. You probably read that on 9 November 1923 the German *völkisch* faction claimed: 'The Kahr Episode does not belong to German but to Jewish history...' 'Kahr's kiss of Judas.'[57] You probably also read that Cardinal Faulhaber, in every way an outstanding figure, was called a 'lackey of the Jews', because he could not, while being true to his convictions, approve of the Hitler undertaking.[58]

The conclusion that a Jewish editor represents Jewish interests in his paper and so publishes a 'Jewish paper' is as senseless as the conclusion that Voltaire's writing belongs to Catholic literature because he was originally Catholic, or that Bebel[59] should be counted as part of the Protestant church because he came from a Protestant family. What do the *Berliner Tageblatt* and the *Frankfurter Zeitung* have about them that is specifically Jewish? The fact that the *Berliner Tageblatt* and the *Frankfurter Zeitung* both came out in full force against the Versailles Treaty, that they oppose Poincaré's policies with unprecedented force? These things are never referred to, but instead something or another is identified that somehow is not popular with certain political circles, and these papers are then labelled as 'Jewish newspapers'.[60]

Undoubtedly there are certain characteristics of the Jewish spirit which I too might not find pleasant. It would be extraordinary if it were otherwise. Jews spent hundreds of years in the ghetto. They got out of the ghetto and into the light about 100 years ago. It would go against every cultural-historical experience if certain characteristics had not developed through the continual isolation of the ghetto, part of which was a one-sided literary preoccupation: the need to be critical, an excessive pleasure in criticizing, characteristics which I also battle against.

I am by no means an admirer of every modern theatrical

production. Recently I allowed myself to be persuaded
to see a production at the Berliner Theater which was
immoral and repellent. I do not know whether the author
or director are Jewish or not. However, I will not visit
such a low play again. Everyone should take that attitude.
In any case, on the one hand we see Schnitzler's *Reigen*
– on the other the Christian playwright Lautensack's
Pfarrhauskomödie.[61] On the one hand you see certain allegedly Jewish theatre directors who take the sanctity of art
lightly, and on the other hand a certain Christian but also
Jewish audience which sadly tolerates such things. But to
insist absolutely that it is characteristic of Jews to propa-
gate such productions and perform them with a definitely
stated purpose (namely to corrupt the Germanic morality
of the German people) – that goes far beyond justice.

When the revolution of 1918 began, the drastic changes
also affected German theatre. There were few Jews among
the leading theatrical personalities – especially not at any
court or municipal theatres, which make up about eighty
per cent of German stages – yet the outcry against particular plays before 1918 was exactly the same as today.
But who, on the other hand, were the personalities who
raised the German theatre to particular regard? The Jew
Adolf L'Arronge founded the Deutsches Theater in Berlin,

for many years acknowledged by all as the best German playhouse.[62] The Jew L'Arronge was followed by the Jew Otto Brahm, and the reputation of the Deutsches Theater, which these men established, was elevated still further by Max Reinhardt – and all these men were Jews![63] And one should not – as is sadly happening – forget the deceased director of the Schiller Theater, Raphael Löwenfeld who, apart from being Germany's leading expert on Tolstoy, introduced the first 'worker's performances', the Sunday morning performances where one could experience the great German and international playwrights – the play-wrights of world literature – for very little money.[64] One must also not forget the sensitive poet Jacobowski, who created low-cost editions of the classics and who published the *New Lyric Poetry for the People* and distributed it to the large circles of the salaried and working class at ten pennies per copy.[65]

Before I close, I must share something with you that is, so to speak, 'confidential'. Reluctantly. For one does not like to speak about the achievements of one's co-religionists. But when it is claimed again and again that German Jews act only in subversive ways, so anti-German, so wearing and trying, you may permit me to recall a series of outstanding men who are Jews and who have achieved great things on behalf of the German people. In the field of medicine, let us recall Paul Ehrlich, who battled against and made groundbreaking discoveries relating to syphilis.[66] Albert Fraenkel, who discovered the pneumococcus, the cause of lung infections.[67] Hehnle [*sic*] of Würzburg, Neißer, Wassermann and, most recently, let us recall the first Nobel Prize winner of Germany since the war, Professor Otto Meyerhof of Kiel.[68] If you review the fields of the natural sciences, chemistry, technology, you will first of all come across the man who was recently awarded the Pour le Mérite in the civil class for scientific achievements, Professor Willstätter of Munich, who discovered chlorophyll, which colours plants green; and Heinrich Hertz, who discovered electrical waves, without which telegraphy and radios would not be possible; and finally Einstein, that ingenious mathematician.[69]

And if one says that Jews cannot be explorers, let me name Dr Kaiser, the first Governor of the Protectorate, the explorer of the North Pole, Bessels, and a man known to all of you at least since your school days, Emin Pasha, who was a Jewish doctor called Schnitzler from Oppeln who, along with Stanley, is one of the heroes of African exploration.[70]

In the field of philosophy, Hermann Cohen and Georg

Simmel distinguished themselves. In literature, a man who was praised in the highest terms even by the *Deutsche Tageszeitung* also stood out: Friedrich Gundolf, about whose work, *Shakespeare and the German Spirit*, it wrote on 1 July 1911:

'A pure historical spirit blows through the work, a deep, humble awe before all things great and beautiful, a rare and noble cast of mind, an aristocratic soul and understanding. We have once again a masterpiece of the German spirit.'[71]

Admittedly, the *Deutsche Tageszeitung* wrote this at a time when it was not aware that 'Friedrich Gundolf' was the Jewish Professor Friedrich Gundelfinger from Heidelberg! And the well-known Pan-German Judicial Councillor Claß, writing as 'Einhart', praised the Jewish artist Messel, who he thought was Aryan, and who has recreated in Berlin an architectural style of most noble simplicity.[72]

I am at the end. I have tried to be objective. I have avoided making a value judgement. I have not tried to blind you with quotations, but I have tried to let the facts speak for themselves.

I would be satisfied if I have succeeded in making two things clear to you:

Firstly, Jews are not a unity, they are a multiplicity;

just as colourful, as political, as economically divided as the German people. There is no such thing as a somehow unified, supranational Jewish organization, nor could there be. Secondly, the 'Jewish spirit' is not better but also not worse than the spirit of the environment in which it dwells.

We German Jews do not want antisemites; we also do not want philo-Semites, no lovers of the Jews. We long for 'justo-Semites', fellow citizens who allow justice to be done to the German Jews in return for honest work for the fatherland and the German people, and who do not judge the German Jews according to the newspapers and prejudices, but simply according to those achievements that have a basis in truth and reality.

The German Jews will continue to work peacefully and quietly for the German fatherland. They will not allow themselves to be robbed of their pride in their origins and religion. But they will oppose with all their might anyone who argues that they are not good Germans, that they are 'aliens and foreigners', in the knowledge that they have always done their duty to the fatherland.

Notes

1 Gabriel Rießer (1806–63), a major figure who worked for the emancipation of German Jews. He rejected the demand that Jews convert to Christianity in order to enjoy equal rights and advocated forming organizations and associations to promote and defend Jewish interests.

2 The Central Association was founded in 1893 in Berlin, to represent non-Zionist German Jewry and defend Jews against antisemitic attacks, such as accusations of ritual murder.

3 Wiener uses the term *Radau-antisemiten*. For this, see p. 87, n. 18

4 Johannes Scherr (1817–86), a German novelist, historian and politician who fled to Switzerland in 1849 after agitating for parliamentary reform on behalf of the Social Democratic Party.

5 Adolf von Harnack (1851–1930), German theologian and church historian who wrote pioneering works on the historical Jesus and argued that Greek philosophy tended to obscure some of the earliest and authentic teachings of Christianity. Emil Schürer (1844–1910), German theologian who studied Jewish history of the time of Jesus.

6 A conflict arising from Otto von Bismarck's attempt to subject the Roman Catholic Church to state control; it began in 1871 and was declared over in 1887.

7 Johannes B. Kissling (1876–1928), author of the classic three-volume history of this conflict.

8 Ultramontanism ('beyond the mountains') refers to the belief in the supreme power of the pope. In the course of the *Kulturkampf*, the papacy was declared infallible.

9 Ernst Troeltsch (1865–1923), theologian, historian, sociologist and politician.

10 For Chamberlain, see p. 86, n. 9.

11 Friedrich August Wolf (1759–1824), classicist credited as the founder of philology, which combines literary criticism, history and linguistics.

12 Victor Bérard (1864–1931), renowned scholar, politician and diplomat, famous for work on the geography of *The Odyssey*. François Hédelin, abbé d'Aubignac (1604–76), playwright and translator of Homer.

13 Wilhelm Röntgen (1845–1923), physicist who won Nobel Prize for the discovery of X-rays.

14 Leo von Caprivi (1831–1899), general and chancellor of Germany.

15 August Anton Ludwig von Mackensen (1849–1945), German soldier who fought in the Franco-Prussian War and the First World War. A committed monarchist, his attitude towards the Nazi regime was ambiguous.

16 The full title is *Semi-Imperator: A Genealogical, Racial-Historical Account to Warn the Future; A Gripping Commentary on the* Semi-Alliancen *in Particular and on the Revelations of the* Semi-Gotha *in General. A Sequel to the* Semi-Alliancen: *Judaified Hohenzollern* (1919).

17 I have not been able to trace a copy of this. Most sources indicate that this is the same book as the *Semi-Gotha*, or perhaps a kind of enlarged edition of it.

18 The full title is *Semi-Gotha's Genealogical Handbook Of Ari(st)ocractic-Jewish Marriages With Lists of Descendants (Pursuit of Descent). Compilation of All Noble Marriages With Full-Blooded and Mixed Blooded Jewish Women and 18 Pedigrees.* (1914). The significance of the parentheses is unclear.

19 A.M. Cooke, 'Queen Victoria's Medical Household', in *Medical History*, 1980, vol. 4, lists no one of this name.

20 Edgar Bérillon (1859–1948), physician and psychiatrist best known for his work on hypnosis. He believed that all Germans give off a bad smell.

21 Friedrich Julius Stahl (1802–61), conservative politician and political writer. Wiener seems to have been mistaken about his original surname – most sources give it as Jolson.

22　Johann Kaspar Bluntschli (1808–81), Swiss jurist and politician.

23　Eduard Lasker (1829–84), German-Jewish jurist and politician influential in the National Liberal Party; Ludwig Bamberger (1823–99), German-Jewish economist and politician, active in the revolution of 1848 and later joined the National Liberal Party.

24　The Tivoli Congress of the Conservative Party had been held in the Tivoli brewery in 1892 and resulted in the party adopting an antisemitic policy.

25　Posen was a Prussian province from 1848 to 1919. The loss of Posen was imposed by the Versailles Treaty.

26　Kuno von Westarp (1864–1945), German conservative politician. He attended a school in Potsdam that Wiener would later attend. He edited the *Kreuz-Zeitung* and espoused far-right antisemitic policies, although softened his anti-republican stance during the mid-1920s. He was later suspected by Hitler of being part of the assassination plot of 20 July 1944, although no evidence to support this was discovered.

27　The Stein-Hardenberg reforms (or Prussian Reforms) were enacted roughly between 1806 and 1815 and ranged from land reform to military reform and some political reforms. They were broadly of a modernizing and capitalist tendency. Historian Mary Fulbrook has written of them: 'The Prussian reforms neither amounted to a single coherent programme, nor were carried by a close-knit, homogenous group of reformers', and in fact Heinrich Friedrich Karl vom und zum Stein (1757–1831) and Karl August von Hardenberg (1750–1822) personally hated one another.

28　Friedrich August Ludwig von der Marwitz (1777–1837), Prussian nobleman and officer who opposed the reforms. The phrase 'revolutionizing… the fatherland' suggests that the reforms would bring the perceived evils of the French Revolution to German lands.

29　Albert von Rauch (1829–1901), Prussian officer.

30　Albrecht von Roon (1803–79), Prussian officer credited with bringing the German Empire into existence, together with Otto von Bismarck and Helmuth von Moltke.

31　Alexander Herzen (1812–70), Russian political writer and activist, who fought against serfdom and governmental corruption and who argued that 'to look at the end and not the action itself is a cardinal error'. Unsurprisingly, he spent much of his life in exile. He died in Paris.

32 Léo Errera (1858–1905), botanist and Jewish (not Roman Catholic) activist. His book *Russian Jews: Extermination or Emancipation?* was published in English in 1894.

33 Hans Delbrück (1848–1929), German historian and politician; Emil Daniels (1863–1934), German politician and pupil of Delbrück's; Peter Kropotkin (1842–1921), Russian aristocrat, revolutionary and scientific writer.

34 Ludwig Büchner (1824–99), German physician, scientist and philosopher associated with scientific materialism (he was the brother of the playwright Georg Büchner); Jacob Moleschott (1822–93), Dutch physiologist, writer on dietetics and scientific materialism; Karl Vogt (1817–95), German zoologist, geologist and politician associated with scientific materialism; Wilhelm Marr (1819–1904), German writer who coined the word 'antisemitism' and promulgated the idea of 'scientific antisemitism' based on racial arguments rather than religious ones. His best-known pamphlet, *The Victory of Jewry over Germandom* (1879), went through twelve editions in the year of publication.

35 Valerian Savelievich Dovgalevsky (1885–1934), revolutionary, statesman and diplomat.

36 Hans Herzog (dates unknown), professor at Berlin University. The pamphlet comprised responses from a variety of public figures to a question about German patriotism and Communism. Hans Herzog's is the longest response and was perhaps deemed interesting as he was a convert to Judaism.

37 Anon., *La France et le pays rhénan*, Imprimerie Lorraine, no date. At bottom left of the cover are the words 'Xe Armée'.

38 Heinrich von Treitschke (1834–96), German nationalist writer and politician, and advocate of authoritarian power politics, German colonialism and German unification under Prussian might.

39 Eugen Dühring (1833–1921), economist, philosopher and writer who espoused a non-Marxist brand of socialism. Regular targets of his criticism were Jews, Greeks and Goethe. Best known in the English-speaking world as the target of Friedrich Engels's polemic, *Anti-Dühring*.

40 For Roth, see *Prelude to Pogroms?*, p. 62 and p. 85, n. 3. I have been unable to trace this title – Wiener may have given it incorrectly. The book in question is almost certainly *The Jews in the Army: A Statistical Examination of Official Sources*, 1919, by 'Otto Armin', a pseudonym of Alfred Roth's.

41 Hermann von Stein (1854–1927), highly decorated soldier who served as Minister of War 1916–18.

42 Raphael Ernst May (1858–1933), London-born German-Jewish businessman and writer.

43 Dietrich Eckart (1868–1923), co-founder of the German Workers' Party (Deutsche Arbeiterpartei), which later became the Nazi Party. He was a proponent of the theory that Jews stabbed Germany in the back, thereby causing the loss of the war.

44 Rabbi Samuel Freund (1868–1939), rabbi in Hanover from 1907, author of several books. His widow died in Theresienstadt ghetto in 1942.

45 Felix Theilhaber (1884–1956), German-Israeli physician and author. Theilhaber was a dermatologist and most of his books specialized in the study of sexual organs. Arrested in 1933, he fled in 1935 and settled in Palestine, where he established the Kupat Cholim Maccabi health insurance company, which is still flourishing. He wrote a number of books about Jewish participation in the First World War.

46 Paul von Lettow-Vorbeck (1870–1964), soldier who fought in south-west Africa in a campaign remembered chiefly for the first genocide of the twentieth century, against the Herero people (although he was not personally involved in the killing). In the First World War he fought a guerrilla campaign which limited the freedom of action of the British and other forces, which made him a popular hero in Germany. He was not a supporter of Hitler's, although a right-wing nationalist.

47 This refers to the French invasion of the Ruhr in 1923, after Germany failed to make reparations payments.

48 This is probably a reference to the Polish rising in Posen in 1919 and the aftermath of the loss of Posen in the Versailles Treaty.

49 Ernst Berger (1857–1919), Viennese-born painter living in Munich; proponent of orientalist art. Held and later shot in April 1919 after being accused of destroying a poster put up by the short-lived Soviet Republic of Bavaria.

50 Count Anton von Arco auf Valley (1897–1945), German nation-
    alist of Austrian birth, antisemite and monarchist. Assassinated
    Kurt Eisner in February 1919, for which he served four years
    in Landsberg, before being pardoned in 1927. Died in a traffic
    accident. Kurt Eisner (1867–1919), journalist and critic who
    organised the 1918 Socialist revolution in Bavaria and became
    the Bavarian republic's first prime minister. He was shot while
    going to hand in his resignation.

51 Adolf Weißler (1855–1919), lawyer and author, who took a critical
    position vis-à-vis Zionism and did not practise his faith (but was
    not baptized). He wrote a utopian novel in which Jews, Muslims
    and Christians found a way to live in harmony. He took his life
    in June 1919.

52 *The Protocols of the Elders Of Zion* is a notorious antisemitic
    forgery originating in Russia in the late nineteenth century,
    purporting to be the record of a meeting of Jewish elders to lay
    a conspiracy for Jewish world domination.

53 Association of Metal Workers (ed.), *Konzerne der Metallindustrie.
    Eine Darstellung der Entwicklung und des gegenwärtigen Standes der
    großen Konzerne der deutschen Metallindustrie* [*Corporations of the
    Metal Industry: An Account of the Development and Current Standing
    of the Large Corporations of the German Metal Industry*] Stuttgart,
    1923.

54 Alfred Hugenberg (1865–1961), industrialist and far-right polit-
    ical leader. A leader of the German National People's Party, he
    greatly influenced public opinion during the Weimar Republic
    through his media empire, and channelled funds towards the
    Nazi Party and later became a member of Hitler's cabinet for
    a short time. Emil Kirdorf (1847–1938), wealthy industrialist
    known for extreme nationalistic and authoritarian views who
    joined the Nazi Party in 1927, leaving it in 1929 only to rejoin
    in 1934. A close associate of Hitler's.

55 Albert Ballin (1857–1918), shipping magnate, director of the
    Hamburg-America Line, at one time the world's largest shipping
    company. He is credited with the invention of cruise-ship travel.
    Despite being a Jew he enjoyed a cordial relationship with Kaiser
    Wilhelm and married a Protestant woman in a church.

56 Walther Rathenau (1867–1922), industrialist, author and politician
    who served as Foreign Secretary in 1922 and was assassinated

in June of that year. In 1909 he wrote an article entitled 'Our Offspring', in which he stated: 'Three hundred men, all of whom know one another, control the economic fortunes of the Continent and choose their successors from their circle.' This was seized on by antisemites to mean that Jews 'rule the world'. The Nazis later also made much of the sentence, wrenched out of context.

57 Gustav Ritter von Kahr (1862–1934), right-wing monarchist politician who was Prime Minister of Bavaria 1920–21, and later assumed dictatorial powers. Despite his reactionary views he opposed Hitler's Putsch in 1923. He was murdered in the June 1934 'Night of the Long Knives' in revenge for this 'betrayal'.

58 Michael von Faulhaber (1869–1952), an ambiguous figure who sympathised with many aspects of Nazi policy but spoke out against the persecution of the Jews, stressing the Jewish origins of Christianity. The 'Hitler undertaking' refers to Hitler's attempted Putsch in November 1923.

59 Ferdinand August Bebel (1840–1913) was Protestant but converted to Roman Catholicism. However, he is remembered as a leading Socialist, one of the founders of the Social Democratic Workers' Party of Germany [Sozialdemokratische Arbeiterpartei Deutschlands] in 1869. He took a strong stance against the genocide of the Herero in south-west Africa and wrote on the role of women in a future Socialist society.

60 Raymond Poincaré (1860–1934), French statesman, prime minister and president who pursued aggressively punitive policies against Germany after the war.

61 Arthur Schnitzler (1862–1931) wrote *Reigen* in 1897. A controversial play, its theme is sex and social class. The title means 'roundel', which refers to the ten interlocking scenes in which couples have sexual encounters, 'the whore' with 'the soldier', 'the soldier' with 'the parlour maid', 'the parlour maid' with 'the young gentleman', etc. It was perceived as extremely scandalous. Heinrich Lautensack (1881–1919) wrote *Pfarrhauskomödie* [*Vicarage Comedy*] in 1911. It explores the comedic possibilities of a priest impregnating his cook, who goes away to give birth out of the public gaze but returns to find her stand-in also pregnant.

62 Adolf L'Arronge (1838–1908), playwright and theatre manager, founded the Deutsches Theater in 1883, running it until 1894,

when Otto Brahm took over. The theatre retains a leading position in Germany today.

63 Otto Brahm (originally Abrahamson, 1856–1912) ran the Deutsches Theater until 1904 and introduced a naturalistic approach modelled on the Théâtre-Libre in Paris. He handed off to Max Reinhardt in 1904. Max Reinhardt (originally Goldmann, 1873–1943), theatre owner, director, film-maker. Reinhardt purchased the Deutsches Theater from Brahm and modernized it extensively. He had brilliant successes, starting with *A Midsummer Night's Dream*, but had to flee Germany in 1933.

64 Raphael Löwenfeld (1854–1910) founded the Schiller Theater in 1893/4. It was one of Germany's first *Volksbühnen* (people's stages), which poor people could attend for low prices. He was the anonymous author of *Schutzjuden oder Staatsbürger? Von einem jüdischen Staatsbürger* [*Protected Jews or Citizens? By a Jewish Citizen*] of 1893. This led directly to the creation of the Central Association of German Citizens of Jewish Faith, the organization for which Alfred Wiener worked, and of which Löwenfeld had been a committee member.

65 Ludwig Jacobowski (1868–1900), poet, journalist and activist. He was a prolific writer who did much to encourage young talent and to make poetry widely accessible. The low-cost books were known as the *Zehn Pfennig Reihe* [*Ten Penny Series*]. He was an active member of the Union for Defence Against Antisemitism.

66 Paul Ehrlich (1854–1915), medical scientist and Nobel Prize winner who did fundamental work on immunology and chemotherapy. In 1909 he and his team discovered Salvarsan, a compound used for the treatment of syphilis until the advent of antibiotics.

67 Albert Fraenkel (1864–1938), physician who, together with Carl Friedländer (1847–87), discovered that some of the bacteria found by Edwin Klebs (1837–1913) in the lungs of people who had died of lung infections were in fact the cause of death – the *Streptococcus pneumonia*.

68 Friedrich Gustav Jakob Henle (1808–85), pathologist who made numerous anatomical discoveries and argued cogently for the germ theory of disease. Albert Neißer (1855–1916), physician who identified the pathogen of gonorrhoea. August von

Wassermann (1866–1925), medical scientist who devised a test for syphilis and made numerous contributions in the field of immunology. Otto Meyerhof (1884–1951), physician and biochemist who won the 1922 Nobel Prize in physiology or medicine.

69 Richard Willstätter (1872–1942), organic chemist who won the Nobel Prize in chemistry in 1915, for his work on the structure of chlorophyll. Heinrich Hertz (1857–94), physicist who discovered that heat and light are electromagnetic radiations. He proved that electromagnetic waves exist and can move through air.

70 The reference to Dr Kaiser is unclear and it has not been possible to identify him. Emil Israel Bessells (1847–1888), Arctic explorer and author who worked for much of his short life for the Smithsonian Institution. Mehmed Emin Pasha (b. Eduard Schnitzer, 1840–92), African explorer and governor of Egyptian Sudan.

71 Hermann Cohen (1842–1918), philosopher and author of important works analysing Kant's philosophy. He was a co-founder of the Society for the Promotion of the Scholarly Study of Judaism (Gesellschaft zur Förderung der Wissenschaft des Judentums), which took a critical and scholarly rather than religious or ethical approach to Jewish studies. Georg Simmel (1858–1918), sociologist and philosopher who wrote influential works on sociological methodology. Friedrich Gundolf (b. Gundelfinger, 1880–1931), poet and literary scholar, a disciple of Stefan George's. When he was a professor at Heidelberg University one of his students was Joseph Goebbels.

72 Alfred Messel (1853–1909), architect who designed the Wertheim department store, the Pergamon Museum and other German landmarks. For Heinrich Claß, see p. 86, n. 9.

Afterword

The Wiener Holocaust Library

by Michael Berkowitz

UPON HIS DEATH in 1964, Alfred Wiener was hailed in the *New York Times* as the 'founder and director of the Wiener Library, which is recognized as the world's foremost research and information center on Nazi Germany'.[1] While this pithy summary passed muster with the *Times*' editors, it is misleading. The Wiener Library probably was not 'the world's foremost research and information center *on Nazi Germany*', overall, in 1964. The fate of documents seized by the Allies following the Second World War was only partially settled by negotiations over their return to German hands beginning in 1949.[2] In the 1950s an immense trove of captured Nazi records was organized and microfilmed under the direction of Gerhard Weinberg in Alexandria, Virginia,[3] who also wrote archival guides that are historical gems in themselves, found only on the shelves of the United States' National Archives in College Park, Maryland.[4]

During the Second World War, Dr Wiener's Library, with neither an ample budget nor paid informants in continental

Europe, keenly surveyed the broad range of Axis activity. This work, along with its earlier efforts, supplied critical knowledge for the Allies. The British government lacked detailed information about the Nazi regime and military institutions. The Library held 'the only collection of material of a very far-reaching and detailed nature on the Nazis since 1933 and even before, that existed in Britain'.[5]

In addition to serving the Office of War Information and the BBC, it was deeply enmeshed in the Psychological Warfare Division.[6] The Library was somehow able to acquire a variety of publications from Nazi-occupied Europe, including technical and specialised journals concerning the war's impact on social and economic conditions, industry and the administration of Nazi rule. No other institution in Britain was able to secure this vital data.[7]

After the war, Dr Wiener's Library reverted more closely to its original remit: antisemitism and manifestations of discrimination and persecution against those deemed 'outsiders'. The Wiener Library was, however, long the premier institution focused on National Socialism's assault on Jews and other victims (1919–39), its perpetration of 'crimes against humanity' as Hitler launched a racially infused war in 1939, and, beginning in 1941, the attempted genocide of world Jewry under Nazism.

The word 'Holocaust' would not have readily occurred to

a *New York Times* reporter in 1964, even though she (or he) had keen insight into Alfred Wiener. The obituary specified that the Library, located on Devonshire Street, central London, focuses on 'the documentation of racial and religious intolerance in all countries. It contains materials – books, pamphlets, leaflets, newspaper clippings – dealing with apartheid (segregation) in South Africa, the Spanish Civil War, Israel and the Middle East, Jewish emancipation and anti-Semitism.' At the time of Alfred Wiener's death, Yad Vashem in Jerusalem, which was established in 1953, would have been regarded as a specialized but modest research centre and memorial, mainly serving Israeli scholars.[8] The Wiener Library was perceived as unique in possessing a collection of nearly 3,000 first-person accounts from those who had been persecuted by the Nazis.[9]

Christine Schmidt has recently explored the centrality of sociologist Eva Reichmann (1897–1998) in the Wiener Library's systematic collection of personal testimonies and related documents. For five years, with backing from the Claims Conference (the Conference on Jewish Material Claims), Reichmann conceived, administered and participated in the collection of some 1,300 testimonies from survivors and refugees, who recounted their experiences from the 1930s to the 1950s. Newspapers throughout Britain and continental Europe published calls for interviewees. Many survivors heard about the project, and volunteered to take part. Trained inter-viewers – many of whom were themselves survivors – recorded and transcribed the accounts.'[10]

Historians Laura Jockusch, Boaz Cohen, Alan Rosen and others have written about organized attempts to collect testimony from survivors in displaced persons' camps after the war. Samuel Kassow has brilliantly illuminated Emanuel Ringelblum's effort to preserve the Warsaw Ghetto experi-ence through the clandestine Oyneg Shabes archive.[11] Alfred Wiener, however, stands nearly alone in having collected 'ephemera' pertinent to the radical antisemitism sprouting in Central Europe in the wake of the First World War, and metic-ulously gathering data on state terror and group violence until the end of his days.

Alfred Wiener and his family fled from Berlin to Amsterdam in 1933. Most of the original collection was lost. In Amsterdam, he established the Central Jewish Information Office, in part-nership with the Board of Deputies of British Jews and the Anglo-Jewish Association. In 1939, Wiener fled to London, bringing the new collection with him. 'Dr Wiener's Library', as it came to be known, provided documentation for the 1945 Nuremberg International Tribunal.[12] It was rarely mentioned during the proceedings, but some of the most compelling evi-dence presented at the Nuremberg International Tribunal, such as that assembled under US General William J. Donovan (1883–1959), derived from Wiener's collection.[13] The Library's supporting role in the Eichmann trial (1961), in contrast, garnered some attention in the press.[14]

Now known as the Wiener Holocaust Library, located on the western edge of Russell Square, for many decades 'the Library' was a mainstay in Devonshire Street, incorporating the Institute of Contemporary History.[15] The latter, which spawned a successful journal, is notable for integrating Jewish and Holocaust scholarship into mainstream academic history, and for research into modern European history, including the post-1945 period.[16] The Wiener Library also shared space for some time with the London branch of the Leo Baeck Institute (LBI). The LBI, founded in 1955, was (and is) dedicated to the history of German-speaking Jewry, and maintains a London office along with libraries and archives in New York City, Berlin and Jerusalem. It too collects eyewitness testimonies and memoirs.

Situating the current Wiener Holocaust Library in the landscape of its peer institutions, after 1964, is complicated by the presence of the Wiener Library at Tel Aviv University, which might be seen as an estranged sibling or partial clone of the London incarnation. As a response to funding shortfalls and a severe financial crisis in the 1970s, and the burst of enthusiasm for the young state of Israel after its Six-Day War in 1967, Alfred Wiener's successors decided to move the Wiener Library to Tel Aviv University.[17] Although he had opposed Zionism before 1939, after 1948 Wiener accepted Israel, so the idea of his library ensconced in Tel Aviv was not as jarring as some assumed. In any event, academics and administrators at Tel Aviv University sought to rehouse the Wiener Library. This did not quite happen as planned.[18]

A substantial portion of the Wiener Library's collection was microfilmed, and shipment to Israel of its books and papers began in the late 1970s, but was curtailed in 1980. The Wiener Library remained active in London, in large part due to the fortitude of Walter Laqueur (1921–2018), who was a co-director of the Institute for Contemporary History.[19] In the late 1980s and early 1990s Tel Aviv University's Wiener Library gained renown for hosting groups of international scholars for year-long residencies, directed by Professor Shulamit Volkov.[20] Volkov, in particular, enhanced the Wiener Library by turning it into a vibrant research institute.[21] She is also greatly significant, along with historians such as Marion Kaplan, Atina Grossmann and Mary Fulbrook, for advancing the kind of integrative history, merging Jewish history in the mainstream, that Alfred Wiener so desired. Despite earlier tensions, the two Wiener libraries have re-established a working relationship.[22]

*

The publications presented here comprise the fruition of a partnership between the Wiener Holocaust Library and Granta Books. They reflect, perhaps as much as any two documents can, what inspired Alfred Wiener to create his library, and provide a sense of what made the Wiener Library remarkable and vital as a research centre devoted to the origins and history of Nazi Germany's crimes against humanity. Although it is difficult to determine the immediate impact of Wiener's thoughts articulated in 1919 and 1924, these pamphlets illuminate a broad spectrum of concerns that shaped – and continue to shape – the mission of his library.

Notes

1 'Alfred Wiener, kept Nazi data; founder and head of London information center dies', *New York Times*, 6 February 1964, p. 29.

2 Astrid M. Eckert, *The Struggle for the Files: The Western Allies and the Return of German Archives after the Second World War* (Cambridge: Cambridge University Press, 2013), p. 1.

3 Daniel A. Gross, 'A historian who fled the Nazis and still wants us to read Hitler', *The New Yorker*, 30 December 2015, newyorker.com/books/page-turner/a-historian-who-fled-the-nazis-and-still-wants-us-to-read-hitler [accessed 17 June 2020].

4 See Gerhard L. Weinberg, *A World at Arms: A Global History of World War II*, new (2nd, 2005) edn (Cambridge and New York: Cambridge University Press, 2018). Weinberg is among the foremost military historians to integrate the Holocaust into the strategy and tactics of the Second World War. At the University of North Carolina (Chapel Hill), he supervised a generation of scholars, including Doris Bergen and Alan Steinweis, who helped lay the foundation for the current field of Holocaust Studies.

5 Ben Barkow, *Alfred Wiener and the Making of the Holocaust Library* (London and Portland, OR: Valentine Mitchell, 1997), p. 87, citing Louis Bondy.

6 Barkow, *Alfred Wiener*, pp. 86 and 89.

7 Barkow, *Alfred Wiener*, p. 93, citing the 'Big Report' from the period.

8 There was an attempt, which failed, to merge the Wiener Library and Yad Vashem in the early 1950s, which would have moved it

to Jerusalem; see Barkow, *Alfred Wiener*, pp. 129–32. The United States Holocaust Memorial Museum in Washington, DC, including a library, archives and research centre, was chartered in 1980 and opened in 1993.

9   The *New York Times* obituary stated that it was 15,000 accounts; otherwise the obituary was accurate and insightful; 'Alfred Wiener, kept Nazi data', op. cit. See Christine Schmidt, ' "We Are All Witnesses": Eva Reichmann and the Wiener Library's Eyewitness Accounts Collection', *Agency and the Holocaust: Essays in Honor of Deborah Dwork*, ed. Thomas Kühne and Mary Jane Rein (Cham, Switzerland: Palgrave Macmillan, 2020), pp. 134–5; see also Leah Sidebotham, 'Walter Laqueur, 1921–2018', Wiener Holocaust Library Blog, 1 October 2018, wienerlibrary.co.uk/Blog?item=342&retrunoffset=0 [accessed 14 June 2020].

10   Christine Schmidt, ' "We Are All Witnesses" ', p. 124.

11   Samuel D. Kassow, *Who Will Write Our History? Emanuel Ringelblum, the Warsaw Ghetto, and the Oyneg Shabes Archive* (Bloomington, IN: Indiana University Press, 2007).

12   Mary Fulbrook, *Reckonings: Legacies of Nazi Persecution and the Quest for Justice* (Oxford: Oxford University Press, 2018), pp. 189–90.

13   See Donovan Nuremberg Trials Collection, Nuremberg trial transcripts and documents from the collection of General William J. Donovan, Law Collections, Cornell University Law Library, lawcollections.library.cornell.edu/nuremberg/collection [accessed 14 June 2020], entries under 'London'.

14   Ben Barkow, *Alfred Wiener*, p. 139.

15   Barkow, *Alfred Wiener*, pp. 151–56.

16   *The Journal of Contemporary History*; see journals.sagepub.com/home/jch [accessed 15/20/2020].

17   Barkow, *Alfred Wiener*, p. 161.

18   'Library's History', Wiener Library for the Study of the Nazi Era and the Holocaust, Sourasky Central Library, Tel Aviv University, en-cenlib.tau.ac.il/Wiener/history [accessed 14 June 2020]. Concerning the formal reconciliation between the two Wiener libraries, see Barkow, *Alfred Wiener*, pp. 182–3.

19   Leah Sidebotham, 'Walter Laqueur', op. cit.

20 See Shulamit Volkov, 'Antisemitism as a cultural code: reflections on the history and historiography of antisemitism in imperial Germany', *Leo Baeck Institute Year Book*, 23:1 (January 1978), pp. 25-46.

21 Several eminent historians of the Holocaust, such as Gordon Horwitz, Peter Fritzsche and Alon Confino are products of Tel Aviv University's Wiener Seminar.

22 Christine Schmidt, personal communication with the author, 26 June 2020.

The Wiener Holocaust Library

The Wiener Holocaust Library is the world's oldest and Britain's largest collection of original archival material on the Nazi era and the Holocaust. Now based in Russell Square in London, the Library has its origins in the work of Dr Alfred Wiener, who during the 1920s in Berlin, and during the 1930s in Amsterdam, campaigned against Nazism. Wiener gathered a large collection of evidence and information about antisemitism and the persecution of Jews in Germany, before moving his organisation and his collections to Britain in 1939. Since then, the Library's collections have continued to grow.

The Wiener Holocaust Library holds some of the earliest accounts produced by Jewish survivors of the Holocaust, as well as thousands of Nazi documents and photographs, and hundreds of collections of documents relating to the experiences of Jewish refugee families who came to Britain in the 1930s and 1940s. In the twenty-first century, the Library has also acquired a number of important digital archives, including the International Tracing Service archive, which contains millions of Nazi era and post-war documents that are used to trace the fates of victims of Nazi persecution.